Better Single
Than Sorry

♥

Better Single Than Sorry

♥

A No-Regrets Guide to

Loving Yourself

&

Never Settling

♥

JEN SCHEFFT

wm WILLIAM MORROW *An Imprint of* HarperCollins*Publishers*

HarperCollins books may be purchased for educational, business, or sales promotional use. For information please write: Special Markets Department, HarperCollins Publishers, 10 East 53rd Street, New York, NY 10022.

FIRST EDITION

Designed by Susan Yang

Library of Congress Cataloging-in-Publication Data has been applied for.

ISBN: 978-0-06-122807-0
ISBN-10: 0-06-122807-9

07 08 09 10 11 WBC/RRD 10 9 8 7 6 5

To Mom and Dad—

Thank you for your unconditional love

and for always believing in me.

Contents

Contents

Contents

Contents

Better Single
Than Sorry

Introduction

It's time for women to start telling the world—and each other—why it's better to be single than sorry. Yes, it's great to have a boyfriend or a husband, and I'm not suggesting we give up the idea of happily ever after, but I don't believe in settling. There is nothing foolish about wanting to meet a man who gives us that certain feeling in our stomachs—and especially our hearts. We need to stop wasting time dating men we're not completely into just because it makes life easier: no more questions about being single; no more feeling like a third wheel when we're out with couples. We need to stand up to people who think that being single is a curse, or who label us too picky because we don't fall in love with every guy we meet. The truth is, we know what we're looking for and we must never sell ourselves short.

It's no easy task, believe me. Some people seem to dislike me because I'm single. What's worse, they ridicule me because I chose to be this way. In 2003, after a stint on ABC's reality series *The Bachelor,* I broke off an engagement to "one of the country's most eligible bachelors." Two years later, as the star of *The Bachelorette,* I rejected two men who apparently thought I was "The One." I was criticized for my decisions. "She wants to be alone?" people asked in amazement. "Without a man? The horror! Could there be anything worse?" At only 28, I was labeled a spinster by *Star* magazine; Elisabeth Hasselbeck from *The View* remarked that I would be a bachelorette for the rest of my life. A bit dramatic, I know, but I guess I should have expected it, considering the message women hear every day: You're not okay if you're not in a relationship.

When I was growing up, I never imagined I'd still be single at age 30. I also never thought that in a period of only two years, I would have been engaged once and turned down two other proposals. I'm not crazy, and I don't have outrageous expectations. I'm not antimen or antimarriage in the least. In fact, I want more than anything to meet a wonderful man and walk down the aisle with him. It's just that I won't do it with someone who is wrong for me.

HOW I GOT HERE

The reason why shows like *The Bachelor* and *The Bachelorette* are created is because people want to fall in love and get married. I applied to be on *The Bachelor* on a dare, but

I wouldn't have agreed to do it if I wasn't exhausted by the dating scene and ready to find my special someone. As we all know, the problem isn't meeting men, it's meeting the *right* man. According to TopDatingTips.com, 68 percent of people find it impossible or difficult to find someone they really like. If only we could snap our fingers and suddenly our ideal man would appear.

Basically, that's what the show was doing for me: They found a fun, well-bred, good-looking, marriage-minded man with no criminal background and a clean bill of health (mental and physical). All I had to do was fall in love. On national TV. In six weeks. And compete with twenty-four others vying for the Bachelor's affection. It certainly seemed like a long shot, but I figured I had nothing to lose. People have met their mate under stranger circumstances.

I never imagined that a few months later I would be accepting an engagement ring from the Bachelor, Andrew Firestone. He was exactly the kind of guy women go wild for: handsome, charming, and—as if the name didn't give it away—an heir to a massive fortune. Women looked up to me as if I had found the male version of the Holy Grail. Strangers approached me for my autograph and dating advice. I was a guest on *Oprah*. The hopes of millions of viewers were riding on my happiness.

Though we never discussed actual wedding plans, Andrew and I knew that we at least wanted to give the relationship a shot. To do so, I had to leave my life, friends, and job in Chicago—a city I loved—and move to San Francisco. Instead of questioning my impulsiveness, people cheered on my sacrifice. After all, we've been brought up to think being in a relationship is the most important thing in the world. Why would I let this "perfect" guy get away?

Six months later, I had an answer: He wasn't perfect for *me*. We were too different. I bent over backward to fit into his life, but I wasn't getting what I needed from the relationship. I was putting so much pressure on myself to make it work, but at the same time, I yearned to be with someone who simply got me. Andrew wasn't satisfied, either, so we mutually agreed to split. I knew I was giving up some "ideal" life, but I had no choice if I wanted to be happy.

Naturally, when I headed back to Chicago, people automatically assumed Andrew must have dumped me. After all, it seemed only a fool would break up with such a catch. My reputation quickly shifted from suspected gold digger to certifiable lunatic. Some women thought I was crazy to give up a fairy-tale life (their idea, not mine). They wondered how I thought I was going to do any better than Andrew.

The Bachelor producers had a solution. A few weeks after the breakup, they called me to invite me to star in the upcoming season of *The Bachelorette*. The more I thought about it, the more it seemed like the thing to do. The show did work for me the first time, even if the results didn't last forever. Of course, my decision was spurred on by the fact that I was somewhat scared that

I would never meet anyone again. I hate to admit it, but at that time in my life, I was feeling a bit desperate. That is never a good time to make a decision about love.

I went on the show and managed to narrow my field of twenty-five down to two men: Jerry and John Paul. They were seemingly "perfect," but I wasn't feeling any real sparks with either one. If I had been dating these men in the real world, I would have stopped seeing them as soon as I felt the relationship wasn't working. (That would probably mean not returning a phone call. At least now, after rejecting all twenty-five men on the show, I've become an expert on other ways to let a guy down easily.) But because of the nature of the series, I had to date them until the end.

At the final rose ceremony, I turned down John Paul's proposal and said good-bye. Instead of flat out rejecting Jerry's proposal, I decided we should at least try dating until the finale aired three months later; at that point, I'd give him an answer. I figured I'd invested nearly a year in *The Bachelorette*—from signing the contract to handing out the final rose—so I had to give it a chance. Besides, the people around us made me feel like I was missing something about him. My instinct was telling me otherwise, but I was under so much pressure that I foolishly allowed myself to ignore it. I was too worried about regrets and didn't want to think I'd wasted my time.

It was determined that I would answer his proposal on a live TV show the night the finale aired. That evening, when I broke the news that I didn't think we should be together anymore, it didn't sit well with Jerry . . . or much of the general public. I was the first person in nine seasons to leave the show unattached (only three out of eleven couples remain together), but what made my decision even more headline-worthy was the fact that I was rejecting common wisdom: I chose to be alone. I was immediately cast as coldhearted, a man hater, a wretched, callous person. The public treated me with so much scorn that you would have thought I had murdered someone.

How dare I actually wait to find the right person?

GREAT MINDS THINKING ALIKE

Despite the criticism, I knew I wasn't alone. There have never been more single adult women in the United States than there are today. Although the average age of women when they walk down the aisle is 25, according to the U.S. Census Bureau, in 2003, 23 percent of women ages 30 to 34 had never been married—that's up from only 6 percent in 1970. For every person who pitied or vilified me, there were handfuls of others who said, "I would have done the same thing." (Research by the National Marriage Project found that 94 percent of never-married singles agree that "when you marry you want your spouse to be your soul mate, first and foremost.") The people who supported me weren't just my friends, either. These were woman from all over the country. They were un-married, married, divorced, young, old—you name it. I realized if I pulled all of our voices together, we would be loud enough to change the way other people feel about being single. Women need to band together and stick up for one another, not encourage one another to sell out.

Throughout the book, you're going to be hearing stories from and about a variety of women. Some of them (i.e., the desperate ones, or the ones who have settled) will be used as examples of how not to behave, but there are also a number who are happily living by the "better single than sorry" creed.

Let me introduce you to a few*:

Melissa, 27; single: She loves her independence and hates when people pity her single status. "I figure every ended relationship just brings me that much closer to the one that will never end. Some days it's painful, but dating is, if nothing else, an extremely amusing activity. I refuse to put my life on hold because I am single. I try to live life to the fullest, knowing that I'm becoming the person I want to pair with someone equally as fabulous, even if research says my eggs are starting to get anxious."

Andrea, 30; single: Her parents spend sleepless nights worrying why she doesn't have a boyfriend. "Once, I made the mistake of telling them I wasn't interested in getting married until I was older and had my life in order," she says. "You would have

---

* In some cases, names and/or identifying details have been changed.

thought that I told them that I had just shot the waiter. I was immediately subjected to a long, torturous lecture about my pessimistic attitude. I looked around to the other diners, somehow hoping that somebody would intervene. Or adopt me. My parents will never change their attitude, but I'll never date a guy just to get them off my back and subsequently make them happy. In fact, I actually like being single! It is a wonderful, liberating feeling to be so independent and not have to answer to anybody or for anybody."

Andrea is one of the sixteen million adults who have tried their luck with online dating. "As much as I want to write it off," she says, "I have several friends who met their significant others via the Internet—and they're not freaks! If it worked for them, maybe, just maybe it could work for me, too."

Blair, 32; single: By now, almost all of her friends are married, and some are even on their second kids. She's neither depressed nor desperate. "Never in my life have I felt sorry for myself that I didn't have a boyfriend," she tells me. "I can't pretend to like a guy, so the thought of being with someone because I just hated being single is so foreign."

Dawn, 38; single: Though she's approaching 40 and has never been married, she remains optimistic. "When I was younger, I thought I'd be married with a baby in my twenties," she says. "When I hit my twenties, I certainly thought it would happen in my thirties. I started a business at 30, and once I grew into my life, something changed. I started reveling in the achievement, the friendships, and the freedom. It would be great to have a boyfriend and regular sex and be loved, but it's only one facet of life. There's so much more."

Valerie, 32; divorced: She's eager to remarry and start a family, but remains cautious after an unfulfilling marriage. "I think the hardest thing about being single is that I have all this love to give someone and I can't," she says.

Ashley, 37; divorced: A family tragedy led her to reevaluate her marriage—and her relationship expectations. "I settled for my husband because I wanted to be married and I thought he was a good catch—which he was, just not for me," she explains. "At the time, I thought he was the best I could get. As I have gotten more confident and more experienced with age, I realize that I deserve so much more."

LIFE LESSONS

I refuse to sit around and feel sorry for myself (the majority of the time, anyway)—and I don't think any other woman should, either. Dating can be frustrating. It can be exciting but discouraging. But there's nothing worse than being in a bad relationship.

I know from experience how important it is for women to listen to their hearts. (Fifty-eight percent of men and women believe it's more important to follow your heart than your head.) Just because someone else— your mother, a friend, a stranger—thinks a guy is right for you, it doesn't make it true. And just because all of your friends are married, you don't have to race to the altar. A happy ending can't be forced: My friend Brad has been in eleven weddings, and nine of them have ended in divorce. There are no guarantees, but we can turn the odds in our favor.

This book should serve as a guide to living your romantic life with no regrets. It all begins with the belief that you are (to steal a phrase from *Sex and the City*) single and fabulous. So many women are desperate because they're insecure. Our lives should be full with or without a man. We owe it to ourselves to be content. It's important to be surrounded by people and things that make us feel good. Every day I remind myself that I'm a valuable human being who deserves to be happy. If we don't have confidence, we can fall prey to the forces of evil—the people (often parents) and things (friends' weddings) that tempt us to settle.

When it comes to dating, we need to trust our instincts from the first time we meet a guy. While we have to be open to men who don't exactly personify our dream guy (or look like George Clooney), we also don't have to date ones we don't like. I know a lot of women make decisions based on the kiss test: If you can't imagine wanting to smooch a guy, let him go. So what if he's your friend's brother? So what if you're going to hear it from your mother? Nothing feels worse than forcing a romance, trust me.

We're all so eager to fall in love that we make excuses for men because they're handsome, rich, or just what our mothers ordered. Time and again, we sacrifice our own needs and our own happiness because we think a man will complete us. Instead, we need to be standing up for ourselves. We need to take responsibility for our own happiness. If a man won't change, you either get over it or move on.

It takes a lot of heartache to figure out all of this, but we have to remember that even painful splits are worth it in the long run. They teach us so much about our own needs. They open our eyes to warning signs and give us the wisdom to not make the same mistake twice. I've been through so many breakups, and they all felt devastating. I would think, Alone again?! Maybe I'm doomed. But life does go on; the search is not over.

MY MOTIVATION

I've written this book in the name of wasted time and broken hearts . . . and hope. I'm still optimistic that I will meet someone. I want to be married and have a family more than anything in the world. I have moments when I panic and think it will never happen for me. We all get scared and feel desperate, but that's when you need to pick yourself up and focus on what's in your best interest. If marriage is supposed to be a lifelong commitment, it should be okay to take your time to find your perfect match. We just have to keep reminding ourselves, it's better to be single than sorry.

Part One

Unwedded Bliss

Chapter One

Being Single Is Not a Curse

*O*ne night not too long ago, I came home from a night on the town with friends and had a major revelation. I was sitting on my couch watching TiVo'd Project Runway episodes, eating a bowl of Cheerios, wearing mismatched pajamas, and sporting a constellation of zit cream of my face. I didn't have to call anyone. I wasn't expecting a late-night visitor. I looked around and I thought, "I'm all alone . . . and I love it!"

Being single is not a curse. All of the time, I hear women saying, "I *need* a boyfriend." It's the desperate woman's mantra. When you utter these words, you might as well be saying, "I'm really pathetic and nothing really matters in this world unless I have a boyfriend—a man in my life to save me from my wretched existence." Because really, not having a man is a fate worse than death, right? At least if you're dead you don't have to deal with *everyone* around you pairing off.

Wrong.

My life is filled with plenty of things that keep me happy and busy—yes, even without a man. I have a great apartment, a fun job that pays me enough so I can stock my closet with way too many pairs of jeans (hey . . . they *are* necessary), wonderful friends, and family. For me, it's the only time in my life I won't have to be accountable to anyone. I don't have to worry about checking in with someone (or worry about what that someone is doing when they're not with me). I'm not fighting with anyone over the remote—or anything else, for that matter—and I love that I don't have to watch action flicks when I'd rather be watching *Pretty Woman* for the millionth time. I also love that I don't have to keep up with shaving my legs or worry about what I look when I'm lounging around the house. If I gain a few pounds, I'm the only one who notices. Even better, if I spend too much money, I only have to justify it to myself. What do I really have to complain about? Nothing.

And I'm certainly not the only woman who feels this way.

Dawn, a 38-year-old self-employed designer, gushes about her solo life. "Being single has, in certain ways, *enabled* me to have a life—a very selfish life—I love. Of course I still have all of the desires that other women have—of wanting to be loved and in a relationship. But it's not like my life will begin once I meet a man. My life is already running exactly how I want it now, and I spend every day trying to make it more so. I have no issues with going to the movies alone or eating dinner by myself. I love having dinner parties. Being single forces you, in a sense, to build more of a network in the world. If you think about it in the right way and not as something tragic, you can become a much more interesting person."

Valerie, 32, is a divorced fashion executive who dates regularly, but tells me, "I am at my best when I'm single. It's when I'm in the wrong relationship—and there have been several—that I lose my edge and all that made me desirable in the first place." She is hopeful that she will find love again, but not to the point of desperation. "I just live every day," she says. "I can be alone and be happy. I don't dislike myself. If this is it for the rest of my life, it isn't so bad."

Seattle-based Annie, 28, is in awe of the advantages of being single. "It's like a free pass to get out of things!" she says. "You're not expected to show up for every dinner party, engagement party, or festivity because you're the 'wild single friend' who has so many dates and crazy stories. I never have to go to church, pick up the kids, make dinner, or chip in on gifts for people I don't know. I have married friends who now do these things—and more."

Literary agent Liz, 27, has been married for two years and looks back at her bachelorettehood not as a dark period, but as a valuable experience. "I enjoyed being single, and now that I'm married, I think that the longing for a steady relationship and the curing out of bad dates is really an important rite of passage," she says. "It's easy for people to lose track of the fact that their lives are a span. It's easy to feel like the kid in the backseat of a car during a long road trip and think that this is the longest trip ever, when, of course, they've only been there for a couple hours. Don't miss out on the fun of being single by getting so obsessed about reaching another state."

PARTY OF ONE

Now, I'm not going to lie and say it wouldn't be nice to have a boyfriend. I want to fall in love, get married—the whole fairy tale. And every once in a while, I panic, whine, and annoyingly ask my friends, "What if I *never* meet anyone? I know you say I will, but what if I *don't*?" (Hey, even the best of us have our moments.) But after I calm myself down, I remind myself that I do not *need* a man in my life to be happy. I've figured out how to take care of that on my own.

What's the secret? Being optimistic and reveling in your freedom. There's no reason to feel pathetic if you have a fulfilling life. A friend once told me that a man should be the icing on the cake, not the cake itself. I refuse to sacrifice all of the benefits of being single—that is, my happiness—for a guy who isn't worth it. I don't have a boyfriend for a good reason: Settling just isn't an option. I gain strength by knowing there are other women out there who agree with me.

At 26, Washington, D.C., attorney Daniele is at the point where many of her friends are settling down, but she's managing to keep a positive outlook. "In some ways, being single is a blessing," she says. "It gives you time to focus on yourself, to discover and grow. Plus, it gives you time to assess whether marriage is even for you." San Francisco–based Dina, 24, isn't letting family pressure taint her perspective on the single life. "I am Russian-Jewish," she explains. "My parents, and all my Russian friends' parents, were married and had kids by the time they were my age. My grandmothers especially can't wait for me to be married and start making grandchildren for them. But I really enjoy being single. I enjoy dating. I enjoy having time for my friends and not being tied down to anything or restricted by anything."

Media executive Heather, 43, isn't fazed by the fact that she's never been married. "I don't think it's great being single, nor do I hate it. I choose to live in the moment and continue to do things with or without a partner. I live my life and I hope that I will find a partner who will want to be on a journey with me. If not, then I will journey alone. My friends are my second family regardless of whether they are married or single. I do believe we have many potential partners out there, and I still believe I will meet someone."

After being in a relationship from ages 21 to 24, Melissa has spent the last three years boyfriend-free. "The last three years in the dating world have played an incredibly important role in my life journey," she explains. "Not only have I discovered who I truly am, but I have become more confident, less uptight, and more attuned to what I truly want out of a relationship. I have formed lasting friendships and taken care of myself by focusing on my career, getting my master's degree, and buying my own place. When I finally meet the right person, I will know that I am the best me possible and will truly be ready to move forward into the next chapter of my life, with no regrets."

YOU DON'T NEED A GUY
TO COMPLETE YOU

There are a few reasons why woman feel like being single is a curse: We're made to feel that way. Just a couple of weeks ago, my dentist said to me, "You're single? How can you be single? I can't believe you can't meet someone!" I know he was trying to give me a compliment, but once he left the room, the hygienist whispered, "Don't let him get to you . . . it's okay!" Questions like that are hard to hear and they're harder to answer. It was as if he thought something was wrong with me—like I was doomed.

Don't let yourself fall into this trap. You don't need to be in a relationship to be considered whole. That *Jerry Maguire* "You complete me" thing? I hate it. No woman (or man) should feel incomplete because they're not in a relationship. Complete yourself.

This reminds me of a funny story I heard from Annie. "I had a post-breakup conversation with a coworker once," she recalled, "and I was telling her how I wanted to marry my ex, settle down, you name it. She asked me, 'Why?' My answer was, 'Well, I want to buy a house, have nice things, and not have to worry about my roommates trashing any of it.' Then I stopped in my tracks and said, 'Wait a minute, I don't want a husband; I want a better job!' It was a very awakening moment."

Since there's no set schedule for when you're going to fall in love, don't sit idly waiting for a guy to come around. Being single shouldn't stop you from doing *anything*. Pursue your interests—yes, even shopping and working out count—and create a life that you'll enjoy even while you're "without boyfriend."

I have friends who have become home owners by the age of 30. Traditionally, most people hold off until they're married (or at least in a committed long-term relationship) to put down roots, but if you have the money, why wait? According to the National Association of Realtors, unmarried women purchased 21 percent of the homes sold in 2005. (Single men bought only 9 percent.) The women I know felt a huge sense of accomplishment because they did it on their own; they didn't have to wait for a man. "I bought my first apartment when I was 28," New Yorker Shannon, now 33, tells me. "The guy situation was never a thought. I knew I wanted to have that for myself—it was a good deal and I could build equity."

And the thought of waiting for a guy never should be what limits your choices or actions. If I want to see friends who are married, I don't mind being the third wheel. I don't let it make me feel depressed. Some of the best times I have are with my friends and their husbands and boyfriends. In fact, sometimes I think the guys feel like they are the third wheels around *us*.

I never hesitate to ask my friends to take a girls' vacation—and there's also nothing wrong with going away alone. "When I was 27, I was in a dead-end relationship with someone who wasn't giving me the time of day," editor Sarah D., 30, remembers. "Even before it all went sour, I took a vacation by myself to Costa Rica. I planned a four-day tour, plus a few days to hang out at the beach, go see volcanoes, and drive around the country. The fact that I was thousands of miles away from him, soaking up sun and surrounded by beautiful things, took my mind completely away from the guy. I came back relaxed, confident that I'd been by myself and had learned so much about the world, and I just didn't care as much for him."

No matter where I am, I make the most of my alone time. It's something I know I'm going to miss when I'm in a relationship. "When I was single, I did a lot of stuff alone," says newlywed nonprofit worker Rebecca, 33, who took a job at a farmer's market as a way to meet people and indulge her passion for flowers. "Now, I actually feel like being in a couple is a bit stifling."

Some women join coed sports leagues—for the exercise and the mingling. When I signed up for a pottery class, I did it just because I thought it would be a fun thing to do. My mom, however, said, "Pottery? You're not going to meet a guy there." Not *everything* you do must revolve around finding your future husband. (Although, you never know—your teacher or classmates could know a nice guy for you. Once, I let my kickboxing instructor set me up—with good results.) It's perfectly fine to participate in activities that are just for you. And that includes spending a quiet night home alone. When my mom worries and says, "How are you going to meet anyone sitting alone at home on your couch," I just blow that off. I *enjoy* watching TV. Just because I'm not at a bar trying to meet men doesn't mean I'm sitting on my couch crying and eating Ben & Jerry's.

CHOOSE YOUR FRIENDS WISELY

Some women are lonely when they're single, but that doesn't have to be the case. I have a wonderful group of close-knit friends—something all single women should focus on cultivating. They draw you out of the house, they boost your morale, and they're your family away from home. And they *get* you better than any guy ever could. Every few weeks, I arrange a girls' night out—no husbands or boyfriends (or calls to either) are allowed. Our only concern is just to be with one another, reconnect, and maybe spend two hours discussing Brangelina (which isn't as exciting—or even possible—with a guy). These nights remind me that even when I don't have a man in my life, there are still plenty of fun things to do. I mean, I certainly don't need a boyfriend to go to nice restaurant.

When I'm with my girlfriends, I don't feel like I'm missing out by not having a man in my life—except when I'm with the few who can't cope with not having a boyfriend. These self-loathing singles focus too much on finding a guy and not enough on enjoying the journey. They're the ones who won't even meet up with their own girlfriends if there isn't also an assortment of men on the premises. "I called a friend of mine once to see if she wanted to meet us out for a drink," recalls investment manager Catherine R., 29. "And her response was, 'Are there any guys there?' I was so offended because I wasn't good enough reason for her to come out."

When I used to socialize with my friend Kelly, 28, she was more interested in scoping the scene than talking to me. I quickly realized she was only using me so she didn't look like a loser trolling for guys all alone. Whenever I'd invite her for a girls' night out, it was a disaster if, God forbid, a guy talked to me or one of our other girlfriends. "What's wrong with me? Why don't they want to talk to *me*?" she'd whine. If we didn't meet a guy by midevening, she'd spend the rest of the night in tears, and we'd have to console her.

Anxiety can be contagious. Occasionally, my other friends and I found ourselves questioning our own worth. If Kelly thinks her life is over because she doesn't have a boyfriend, does that mean she thinks we're losers, too? I had to ease myself out of that friendship. To be okay with being single, you have to surround yourself with positive people who don't bring you down.

There are so many women out there like Kelly, who are so stressed about dating and marriage that they lose sight of all of the goodness in their lives—and themselves. I just want to shake some sense into them.

Three things worry me most about these types of women:

+ By spending all of their free time obsessing over men (that they don't even have), they're cheating themselves out of this time in their lives when they should be making the most of their freedom.
+ If they hate being single, they're going to lower their standards.
+ They constantly set themselves up for disappointment.

If you love yourself, you won't fall into any of these traps.

BOTTOM LINE

Because it's so great to be single, I don't have to stress about not having a boyfriend. There's no need to make myself crazy. If I meet a guy and something does happen? Great. If it doesn't? It's his loss, not mine. I already have a wonderful life.

Chapter Two

. . . .

It Takes Guts to Be on Your Own

*T*here are times *when I get down about being single," non-profit worker Becky, 30, tells me. "Sometimes, I wonder how long it would take for people to realize I was missing. I mean, how old do you want to be when it's still your mother who realizes that? Also, every year on Valentine's Day I get flowers. For about thirty seconds, I think, Maybe it's from a secret admirer . . . but it's always my dad. I wonder, When is it going to be someone else?"*

People always say relationships are hard, but being single is also a challenge. I've watched as most of my friends have paired off. I have people constantly asking if I have a boyfriend. ("If you report your status as single-and-fine-with-it," notes editor Melissa, 27, "you get the verbal equivalent to a pat on the head and a sappy smile of pity.") I'm constantly facing pressure from friends, family, and even society to be in a relationship. I'm okay being alone, but for those who can't stand it, just getting through the day can be difficult.

Women who get married are applauded for landing a guy, but women who are single—including those who call off engagements and marriages—deserve the same respect, if not more. The truth is, most of us could be married if we really wanted to be. (I should know; I've been proposed to three times.) It's just that we've made the choice not to settle—something so many people can't seem to understand.

It takes a strong woman to hold out for the *right* guy when the rest of the world seems to be telling you you're *wrong*. For the past few years, that has been the story of my life. As a result of my *Bachelor* and *Bachelorette* break-ups, I experienced criticism so far beyond what any other woman has had to withstand. Do a Google search for my name and you'll find a host of insults: "Jen is out for Jen. She's in love with herself. How could she possibly fit someone else in?" and "Actually saying Jen Schefft, the current *Bachelorette,* is a bitch is putting it lightly." Detractors dubbed me "Idiotic Bimbo," "the most despised reality TV character of all time," and an "attention-getting whore."

People also dug up my work e-mail address and flooded my in-box—and those of my colleagues—with messages about how awful they thought I was. Meanwhile, my parents received letters from angry viewers telling them I was a horrible person, that I obviously had no idea what I wanted in a man, and that I was never going to be happy. Two months after the show aired, a woman even approached me in a store and said she was really worried about me and recommended I seek professional help.

Because I broke up with Andrew and Jerry, strangers automatically assumed I had a lot of issues, or that I was impossible to please—as if there weren't two people in these relationships. They could only see the superficial aspects of what I was giving up: two great-looking men (one of whom had a large family fortune). I was forced to defend myself for being single when all I really was trying to do was create a situation in which I would be happy. What's wrong with that? We shouldn't feel the need to apologize for depriving *other* people of the fairy tale.

Even though my situation was unique (most people don't have to worry about disappointing millions of fans when their relationships fail), my pre-breakup concerns were nothing out of the ordinary: I was terrified of what our families (especially Andrew's, who were my employers at the time) and friends would think. I was nervous that cynics would hiss, "I told you it would never work." No one wants to admit they care about other people's opinions, but you do; it's human nature. I found myself wondering, Am I crazy? Am I making a good decision? Will I regret this later? Naturally, I was also freaking out about having to start the dating process all over again. (Please, not another awkward setup.)

But I had to do what was best for *me*. I mustered up

the nerve to face my fears, I asserted my independence, and I walked away. A friend of mine joked that it reminded her of the classic *Beverly Hills 90210* episode in which Kelly is forced to decide whether she wants to accept boyfriend Brandon's marriage proposal or take a trip around the world with former love Dylan. After careful consideration, she tells them, "I choose *me*."

Still, choosing yourself isn't always as simple as it sounds. If there wasn't so much pressure for women to be in relationships, I would have quickly come to terms with the fact that I was totally incompatible with Andrew and Jerry. Instead, walking away required an enormous amount of courage. Why? As author and family therapist Terrance Real explains, "Women are taught to filter their sense of well-being and worth through a relationship."

THERE GOES THE BRIDE

Whenever I hear a story about a woman my age getting divorced or calling off an engagement, instead of feeling sorry for her, I'm impressed. Don't get me wrong, it's not because I think it's great to get divorced. (That's one reason why I'm taking my time finding my husband.) I just know how difficult it is to walk away from that dream of happily ever after.

Not too long ago, my friend Veronica, 30, called off her wedding. It was three months before the Big Day. It wasn't as if she'd rushed into anything: She and Chad were together for seven years; an engagement seemed like a logical next step. Planning for the wedding, however, quickly became a nightmare. She hated every aspect of it. Nothing was ever right for her, from the invitations to the bridesmaids' dresses. She never even got excited about going wedding dress shopping. (Once her gown arrived, she didn't even want to pick up.) It was obvious to all of us that she wasn't happy about the wedding.

By the time she decided not to walk down the aisle, the save-the-date cards were already out. Her parents had put down thousands of dollars in nonrefundable deposits. The bridesmaids had shelled out $300 for something we'd likely never wear again. (As a friend, I'd gladly sacrifice that bit of cash compared to the money and heartache Veronica would have had to put into an actual divorce.) She felt so badly about disappointing anyone. "I had so many sleepless nights," she told me a few weeks later. "I was giving up something that every woman dreams about. It was agony coming to terms with this decision. But they tell you that deep down 'you know,' and I didn't know." She was afraid her parents would be furious, but as it turns out, they weren't angry at all. "I'm not *mad* at you," her father told her. "I'm *disappointed for* you." There's no question that it would have been a lot easier for her to walk down the aisle than to tell everybody she didn't want to go through with it. She would have crossed her fingers and sucked it up. Not the ideal way to enter a marriage. As time passes, she's even surer that she made the right choice—and she's incredibly proud of herself.

"It takes a tremendous amount of courage to call off a wedding," says NYC wedding planner Ann David of David Reinhard Events. "The bride has made a public commitment. For her to go back on that very sacred and important decision and have to tell friends and family—that's a very difficult thing to do. But you need to follow your heart and do what is best for you. It is an unfortunate situation, but it is better to realize this before the wedding."

I know of a few women, however, who came to that realization a little too late. My friend Ashley, 37, spent four years in an unhappy marriage, and, sadly, it took her father's death to give her the motivation she needed to break free. "When my dad was dying, we had a talk one day, and he told me he didn't regret one minute of his life because he knew he had been with the right person—my mother, who made him so happy. That made me reevaluate *everything*," she explains. "My marriage was empty, a business agreement. My husband didn't love me the way I needed to be loved." And still, people thought she should stay in it. "People *who didn't really know me* told me I was nuts for leaving," she recalls. "They figured because I had a nice house and a fancy car and I didn't have to work—and dating is 'so hard'—it would be stupid to leave." As painful as it was, she's learned so much about herself and how she wants to spend her future. "I would rather be alone than with the wrong person again," she says. "Trust me, being in a miserable marriage is much worse.

On some level, I feel like my dad died so that I could be happy."

Divorcée Valerie went through a similar experience. She lived in a big house in the suburbs, drove a BMW, owned a dog—it was everything she'd always wanted. Or so she thought. A little more than a year after her wedding, she realized she had made a terrible mistake and decided to leave her husband. "When we separated, I left everything," she says. "It took guts to walk away from that—to walk away with nothing and start over in every sense. My parents were supportive, but not really. My father wanted me to make the 'adult decision,' which in his mind would have been to stay and fight. He says, 'At its best, marriage is tough.' And he's right. But I think he thought I was backing down from the fight. It wasn't like that. I knew in my heart of hearts it wasn't a situation to bring children into, and that was what I wanted. Finally, it came to a point where nobody else had to be okay with it but me— and I was. Every day is tough being single, but my favorite thing to say is that being happy is tough. It's a job. You really have to work at it. And to be completely happy, you can't be in a relationship because it's convenient."

It took real estate developer Fay, 40, three and a half years to build up the strength to leave her husband of ten years—even though he had cheated on her *four times*. "Before I could do it," she explains, "I wanted to be happy with *me*. I had to find confidence in myself. I am worthy of love and everything I deserve. Now, I'm excited for the future."

SELF-RELIANCE

As much as I love the freedom of being single, I also love the sense of security, constant companionship, and affection that comes with being in a relationship. I'm not too proud to admit I yearn for those things once in a while. And when I'm in a relationship—even a bad one—those are the forces that keep me tied to the other person (not to mention that our lives are often completely intertwined). That's why it can often seem so much easier to stay in relationships than to leave them. *Desperate Housewives* star Eva Longoria once said she was going to be with her boyfriend Tony Parker forever because she's "too lazy to look for someone else." And that's coming from someone who could probably have almost any guy in the world.

Don't fall into this trap. Laziness is not the key to happiness, and neither is being with someone just for security. For example, my friend Janet, 30, couldn't stand living by herself. She had gone from living with her parents to sharing an apartment with roommates. "I like to feel like someone is taking care of me," she admits. When the time came for her to get her own place, she couldn't handle it, so she convinced her boyfriend, Rob, that they should move in together. Well, actually, he barely had a say in the matter. In fact, he never even told his parents she was living there. Now, her relationship is failing but she's staying in it. She confesses, "I just don't want to be by myself."

According to Dennie Hughes, author of *DateWorthy* and "RelationTips" columnist for *USA Weekend,* there's a good reason why women like Janet are so scared. "Our society is all about not being alone," she says. "They tell us, 'You need to find someone to take care of you. You're not getting any younger. You *need* to have children because you need them to take care of you when you get old.' Women need to fight this."

I've learned that being in a bad relationship can be even lonelier than being single. When I'm not getting what I need from a man, I feel unimportant, unloved, and neglected. Plus, it's stressful to be constantly fighting and worrying about what you're saying or doing. I'd rather be alone. These days, Janet and Rob don't even hang out; they're not even friends. Yet, she's keeping him around so she doesn't go to bed alone. What I keep telling Janet is Rob's role in her life shouldn't only be as a security blanket. Get a dog. Live in a building with a doorman. Find a roommate. Grow up and learn to take care of yourself. "Men don't live as long as women," says Hughes. "You have to face the fact that at some point you are going to be on your own." Even though you're giving up the companionship, you're getting control of your own life in return. I feel such a sense of accomplishment when I look around *my* apartment and see *my* things and know that I've been able to get to this point on my own.

FLYING SOLO

. . . .

Whether you're a serial single or just coming out of a relationship, you have to be prepared for two things: to have your self-esteem tested and to put up with people thinking you're [*insert derogatory term here—I'm sure I've been called them all*]. Remember, your weapons are your confidence and your guts. No matter what people have said about me (or how many times I have wished I had a boyfriend), I have never second-guessed myself or any of my decisions. I've even gotten used to doing things alone: If I have an urge to see a movie or go out for dinner and no one is available to join me, I'll still do it. I'm not worried about anyone looking at me and saying, "How sad."

Attending weddings, reunions, and formal events alone, however, can be even harder than asking for a table for one. When you're invited with a guest, RSVPing can lead to mini anxiety attacks. My company e-mailed our holiday party invitations, and at the top were two boxes where you had to check off if you were bringing a guest or coming ALONE. (I swear, it really was capitalized.) Even when you're surrounded by friends at a party, being the only single person can feel uncomfortable. "I was at a wedding and I was seated at a table with four couples," says single writer Blair, 32. "Everyone was talking to their dates, so I had no one to interact with. And I didn't want to intrude. When they would all get up to dance, I'd be left alone. Sometimes, a pair would ask me to join them. I wanted a dance partner, not a threesome. I felt like such a charity case."

As New Jersey–based Melanie, 28, learned, even buying an apartment—something that any uncoupled woman should be proud to do—affected her self-worth. "I was forced to sign documents with 'Melanie Redout, unmarried' centered, capitalized, and bolded at the top," she remembers. "My attorney explained that it was to prove that only I can claim ownership of the property, but it felt like even the state of New Jersey was rubbing it in!" She should be glad she doesn't live in England. Up until 2004, the word *spinster* was the legal term for a single woman, regardless of age.

You don't even have to be unattached to feel like a second-class citizen. Just being unmarried can be difficult, as consultant Sarah B., 33, learned when she attended a retirement party for her father. "I had been dating Scottie for just over a year," she recalls. "I was pretty confident about our relationship and glad to talk about it. But no one even asked! They were more interested in my married sister and her new baby. It was as if people didn't seem to think I was a valid person because I wasn't married. It hurt." She didn't let it get her down. "I said, 'Screw it,' and moved on," she explains. "I didn't internalize it because there wasn't much I could do about it. It's funny though, no one really believes that story unless they are in a similar situation."

I get it. That's how I feel every year around Valentine's Day. I hate that holiday even when I'm in a relationship.

But when I'm not, I get the feeling that everyone in the world is part of a couple, and everything in the world is designed just for them. It's as if unattached people don't even exist. It's the one day, where if you're already depressed about being single, you might as well kill yourself. Okay, maybe it's not *that* bad. But it is stupid, and all it does is make single women feel worthless.

Incidents like these can be humiliating and embarrassing and make you want to run off with the next guy you meet. But don't do it. Stop feeling sorry for yourself. Think about the things you have to be happy about. You're worthwhile even without a man in your life. Not every situation you're going to be in will be comfortable. Deal with it.

STAY STRONG

When I'm single, nothing is harder than a Sunday. To me, that's a boyfriend day. That's when you sleep in, you relax, and you just hang out and cuddle. It's hard when you don't have that. But there's no reason to spend that time sitting around feeling sorry for yourself. Use the day to visit friends and family (as long as they won't harp on your singleness), run in a race for a charity, or take a class—anything to ward off wallowing. "My girlfriend Mo and I go out to our favorite watering hole every Sunday night and talk about what's been going on and the week to come," says marketing director Lea, 33. "We bill it as a 'self-promotional' night. We can only say positive, good things about each other—and pump each other up."

Here are some other tips to give you the strength to stand on your own:

If your friends in couples don't include you . . .

✦ Don't just sit around waiting for them to call. Initiate the plans for a night out, or invite them over for dinner.

✦ Don't whine. Tell them that you want to be included. Maybe they're worried you'd feel uncomfortable, even if you know that's not the case.

✦ Make an effort to make more single friends.

If you're dateless at an event . . .

✦ Think about how many people got in fights on the way to the party.

✦ Think about bad moments with an ex and thank God he's not there.

✦ Be glad you don't have to worry about making sure your date is having a good time.

✦ Don't be a wallflower. Make it your goal to meet four other people. (You never know who they may know.) Talk to other women or other couples—it's not just about meeting men.

If you're home alone for the holidays . . .

✦ Realize that you won't always have this private time with your family. At some point, you'll be splitting holidays with your in-laws and you'll miss being with your own people.

✦ Be glad you're not worrying if your boyfriend likes your parents or vice versa. There are never any guarantees.

If you don't have a Valentine . . .

✦ Get a group of friends together and go to a place where you won't be surrounded by couples.

✦ Think about all of the women who will be disappointed because the man in their life didn't buy the right gift or make the right reservation, or because he forgot about the day all together.

✦ Act as if it's like any other day of the year—because it is.

BOTTOM LINE

Be proud of yourself for having the courage not to settle. And remember, no matter how hard it might be to be on your own, you can't hurry love.

Chapter Three

Don't Play Hard to Get,
Be Hard to Get

W hen I go out with my single friends, they stand around waiting for something to happen," says married New Yorker Sheila, 29. "Recently, I went to Club Med with a girl-friend of mine—my husband didn't come with us—and I became acquainted with all of the single guests. Even though I wasn't looking for a relationship, my energy said 'Let's meet.' The comfort of knowing that I have someone gave me the confidence to be open to other people. I had a great time. Now I'm the person that all my single friends want to go out with because I attract people."

You're probably wondering why I'm telling you a story about a married woman. It's simple: Sheila was alluring because she knew she had nothing to lose. She wasn't trying to impress anyone, say the right thing, or act a certain way. She wasn't trying to manipulate anyone's actions. She didn't put any pressure on herself. And she knew that at the end of the night, even if she didn't make any connections, it didn't matter because she had someone at home.

I have someone at home, too: MYSELF. And being happy being with that person—that is, knowing I can survive without a man—is the foundation of my approach to dating.

I don't play games because they aren't necessary. This may sound strange, given that I was on a TV show where it seemed my main purpose was to be the one woman out of twenty-five to "win the guy"; however, my only intention was to have a good time and see where things might lead. I was determined to be myself from the beginning and not get caught up in the craziness and the competition. In the back of my mind, I always knew that if it didn't work out with Andrew, I would go back home to a life I loved. While most of the other girls were throwing themselves at him, I didn't go out of my way to be noticed or tell him I was ready to have his babies. I wasn't oozing with desperation. He respected that, and it made him want to get to know me better. Although my so-called strategy was completely unintentional, it worked. I was the one he wanted to be with in the end. I didn't have to manipulate him. The attraction came naturally.

BATTLE OF THE SEXES

I find it funny when girls say they are playing hard to get. "Guys don't even know you're doing it to them," my friend Mack tells me. "We're completely oblivious to things like that." Adds investment banker Roger, "It would turn me off if someone didn't call me back. I'd think she wasn't interested or a flake. Either way is bad." That's not to say men aren't attracted to women who are a bit of a challenge. "Growing up, boys and girls hear the same fairy tales," explains relationship expert Dennie Hughes. "Women hear that they should be waiting for their Prince Charming. Men hear that any woman worth having is a woman worth fighting for." *But the challenge has to be real.* It has to be because of what is going on in your life, not because you're creating this fake-busy persona or following some set of rules. "When a man calls and you have plans, it ups your desirability factor," says Hughes. If you're happy on your own, you're automatically going to *be* hard to get because you're not going to throw yourself at every guy. "I think you meet people when you least expect it," says single Lea. "Wearing your heart on your sleeve makes you an obvious desperado. If you have tons of fun stuff going on, you give off an exciting vibe that makes you more attractive."

After my friend Mandy, 30, an advertising executive, ended a five-year relationship with Michael, all she wanted to do was focus on herself for a change and enjoy being single. "I was doing things and realizing I didn't need Michael or his family around to make me happy," she recalls. "As soon as I was in a place where I didn't need a man—and I also wasn't using all of my effort to find one—guys started popping up. When I met Barry, I was really honest with him about where I was and what I was thinking: I wanted to date other people and spend time with my friends. This allowed me to really get to know him rather than immediately wonder, Is he The One? I think it made me seem 'hard to get'. He made a huge effort to win me over."

RULES SHMULES

Whenever I've tried to follow any of those play-hard-to-get rules—usually on the advice of a seemingly well-intentioned friend—instead of ending up with a boyfriend, I'm left with a massive headache. *Should I reply to his text message immediately? How many hours should I wait to return his call? How many days do I have to wait to see him? Do I have to pretend I'm busy on Friday night? Am I doing this right? Actually, what am I doing??* When I don't like someone, I "let them down easily" (essentially blow them off) by not returning phone calls and hope they'll get the idea. But when I actually do like someone, I'm *also* not supposed to call him back? Talk about mixed messages.

Here are some examples of the difference between playing hard to get and being hard to get:

Playing hard to get	Being hard to get
✦ You're cold and aloof because you think it's mysterious and that's going to make him want you more. (Um, what if he's not attracted to bitches?)	✦ If you're distant, it's only because you have a lot going on and you're not around to call all the time. But when you're with him, you're attentive and show him your best self.
✦ Purposely not returning a guy's phone calls and calculating a random number of hours you're going to wait until you do so. "If he called me at 4 P.M., I guess I have to wait at least forty-two hours to call him back so he doesn't think I'm desperate."	✦ Not calling back immediately because you're *actually* busy with work, dinner with friends, a manicure, whatever. But you *can* call back in the same evening. There is such a thing as manners.
✦ He asks you out on a Wednesday afternoon for the following night, and even though you don't have plans, you tell him you won't be free until the following Saturday.	✦ He asks you out and you can't go because you really do have plans. Suggest another day that works for you to let him know you'd still like to see him.

If games aren't necessary, why do women play them at all? Insecurity. Game players don't believe they have enough to offer on their own, so they try to do things they think make them seem more appealing. Admits investment manager Catherine R., "Thoughts go through my head: I don't want to appear like I don't do anything and I'm not a busy person because I am. I have a full life. I don't want to appear as if I'm waiting with bated breath by the phone. But I try to keep those thoughts in check and tell myself, If I want to see the guy, then I should call him. I've gotten advice from friends like, 'Don't call him back for four days.' But I'm much more interested in a natural flow of interactions. At the same time, if the person I've started seeing wants to see me every other day, even if I really liked him, I wouldn't necessarily agree to that. I wouldn't want to jump into something. I try to take it slow."

Dawn is so beyond playing hard to get that she's learned some men find her intimidating. "An old boyfriend was over the other night and he told me, 'Truthfully, Dawn, you scare men because you say things straight.' He's right. I know what I want and I'm not afraid to tell people. I'm not scary or mean. As a matter of fact, as I've gotten older, more set in my ways, and more confident in who I am, I'm nicer and kinder to men. I'm not as afraid. I know how hard it is to for men and women to connect. But I think the more mature you are and the more okay you are about it, that alone can be intimidating to guys. It's not just because you're accomplished. Being intimidating helps weed out the bad ones, actually. A guy who wouldn't be receptive to that or rise to the occasion and be more grown up about it is not someone I would want to be with anyway. It's the natural selection process. It lowers the numbers, but at least you're getting more quality."

HOLDING BACK

There is a lot to be said for not forcing yourself on someone. Think about it: If a man calls you a million times and you don't call him back, there is a reason. When that happens to me, I cringe every time his name pops up on my phone or e-mail. Reverse the situation and ask yourself, Do you want to be that girl he's cringing at? Never. Plus, men take longer to fall for someone than women do. "Society programs men to hold out," says Dr. Debbie Then, a California-based social psychologist and author of *Women Who Stay with Men Who Stray.* "Men just want to get it right." If you start rushing him, he's going to freak out. If he's interested, he will pursue you. "When I was dating my husband," stay-at-home mom Patty, 33, tells me, "I didn't have to call him once."

When I'm interested in someone, I give him little signs to let him know. In person, I make eye contact and smile. If he calls me, I'll answer my phone. Or if I get a message, I try to call him back as soon as I have a free moment. I'm not worried he's going to think I want to marry him just because I get back to him in a timely manner. (I don't, however, call him fifty times a day.

He'd think I was a freak—and rightly so.) When I'm in that getting-to-know-you stage, I go with what feels right and I don't stress about it. I want to be myself. Even more importantly, I want to just *be*.

Some women I know who are into online dating have a hard time with this concept. If they meet (or at least communicate with) a guy they like, they'll constantly check his profile to see if he's logged on and if he's looked at their profile. Panic quickly sets in if he doesn't send an e-mail every time he's online. "You can drive yourself crazy," says Heather. "Unless you get serious with someone and have 'the chat,' I think you can expect him to be looking and dating online." Chicagoan Lisa, 34, chooses to see a bright side when she notices a guy she likes is surfing the site consistently: "He hasn't met someone else." While online dating can be great, the ability to monitor's a guy's actions is a definite downside. You have to learn to control your curiosity for the sake of your mental health. Think about it: If you didn't meet online, you'd never be able to keep track of a guy to that extent. And that's a good thing.

MAKING MOVES

While dating, there are times when you have to take matters into your own hands. Don't get me wrong, I want to be pursued, and most of the time I let the guy make the first move. But sometimes it's necessary to give a little nudge, like if you see a cute guy at the grocery store, or have a quick conversation on the bus, go ahead, slip him your card. A few years ago, I met a bartender while I was out. This is so unlike me, but I left my number on the bar when I left. Nothing ever came of it, but I wasn't upset because I didn't do anything that embarrassing (like stalk him and show up at the bar every night). I was just happy that I didn't leave regretting anything. Give him enough to know you're interested, then go forward and live your life and see what happens.

"I had a crush on a guy friend, and I found out I had to travel to his town for a meeting," says Blair. "So I sent him an e-mail. It was pretty blasé—something like, 'Hey, I'm going to be around on Thursday, and after my meeting I'm going out with some friends. If you're around, maybe we can meet up.' He didn't write me back immediately, so I started freaking out. But later that day, he called and we had a long talk and made plans to get together. When we finally saw each other, I was still nonchalant about the whole thing. I just wanted to see how things went. We got along well, but I had no idea if he was interested in me romantically. As it turned out, he was! We had a great time that night, and before he went home he invited me to join him for lunch the next day. I guess some people would have told me to say I was busy (which I wasn't), but the fact was, I liked spending time with him. Why deprive myself of that?"

This is why so many friends end up falling in love. There is zero game playing. Neither party is worried about saying the wrong thing or doing the wrong thing. You're acting completely like yourself. You give that person as much time and attention as you want; your actions are not calculated. All the usual dating nonsense—like trying to figure out what it means when he says "Bye" as opposed to "Talk to you later"—doesn't get in the way.

I once dated a coworker, whom I'll call Chris, but it took six months for us to get together. When he first expressed interest, I already had a boyfriend, so the most I could offer was a friendship. We worked closely together and got to know each other without any of the pressure or pretenses that would have come with dating. It was great. Over time, we became close friends. Eventually, my relationship ended, and Chris and I started dating exclusively. It was so nice to be with someone with whom I was already so comfortable. We dated for about a year and a half. Unfortunately, it ended when he moved out of state, but it was one of best relationships I've had.

GREAT EXPECTATIONS

Desperate housewives may be sexy, but a desperate bachelorette is not. Easy-to-get women will often settle for the wrong guy and a bad relationship just for the sake of having a boyfriend. They're so eager to make a connection—to be saved from their lives of misery—that they just can't slow down and ease into a relationship. Women like this jump at every guy who shows interest in them, without even questioning how they actually feel about the guy. They just want a boyfriend so badly that it doesn't matter.

As important as it is to be optimistic about your love life, being realistic is also critical. If there's one thing I've learned over the years, it's that I'm probably not going to meet someone every time I go out; and if I do meet someone, there's a good chance it's not going to work out. What I'm saying isn't meant to sound negative or self-effacing. It's just a fact of life. If I didn't come to terms with it, I'd be disappointed *a lot*. Instead, I am so much happier and less tense than the majority of women I see.

Lori is a 29-year-old journalist in Dallas. Her friends say she's smart and pretty, with a killer body that makes them all jealous. "I think guys like her when they meet her because she's put together," explains one of her friends. "She's smart, flirty, well-dressed. I think she can hold their attention." And yet, Lori spends a big part of her day feeling sorry for herself because she's single. Every time she meets a new man, she's convinced he's going to be The One. "I think guys are initially attracted to her," says her friend, "but then she scares them. I bet when she's on a date she makes comments like, 'All my friends are married.' Or she interviews the guy: 'Do you want to move out of the city? Why are you still single?' She puts herself down. She opens up too much. I can guarantee you she brings up past relationships. She also gets pretty drunk and makes out with guys; she'll take them home on the second date. The desperation must seep through her clothes." If her most recent date doesn't call right away, Lori has a breakdown. "Boys don't like me. What's wrong with me?" she sobs to her friends—that is, the few left who will listen. She threatens to leave town or get (totally unnecessary) plastic surgery. She considers herself a complete failure and says she never expected her life to turn out this way. "I don't like to be around her," confesses her friend. "There's no reasoning with her."

According to Beverly Hills psychotherapist Dr. Jenn Berman, "No man wants to be with a woman who is depressed and unhappy with her life and unsatisfied." I guess you're lucky if you find someone who feels that way, too. But odds are you're going to turn off more people than you're turning on. "A guy who is looking to sleep with you is going to be totally freaked if you say you're ready for marriage. That guy will run for the hills."

Don't be afraid of being rejected—and don't take it personally when it happens. You don't make friends with every woman you meet, so what makes you think you're going to hit it off with every man? My friend

Olivia, a 31-year-old sales manager, says online dating helped her become a casual dating expert. (This was before she met her current boyfriend on a matchmaking site.) "I got into the mind-set that this was going to be fun and I'd just see what happens," she explains. "I was excited about going out, but I stopped having expectations that one guy would be The One because I knew there would be other dates." Plus, if you're not worrying about what a guy thinks of you, you'll be able to act more like yourself on a date. Trying to fit into a mold of what you think he wants lays a foundation of lies for your whole relationship.

Not believing every man I meet is going to be Mr. Right also protects me from getting swept up in some guy's game. I'm naturally cautious, and it saves me from a lot of heartache. Men love to say what women want to hear; they dish out compliments that are often meaningless. "You're so amazing" is one of my favorite lines. You just met me; how do you know if I'm amazing? Because you've seen me on a TV show? Or are you saying that because you think it's going to win me over? When I hear a line like that, or anything similar, I automatically assume he says that to every girl he meets. I don't allow myself to be drawn in.

HOLDING OUT

Being hard to get also applies to sex. Women like Lori are so caught up in rushing things that they'll often hop into bed with someone before they really get to know him. They (mistakenly) think they've found their soul mate and that sex equals commitment. "Sex sells, but sex on a first date sells you short," warns Hughes. "Once you have sex, you never have the chance to go backwards to the courting part. There is something wonderful about dating someone and wondering what they are like."

What desperate women don't understand is that being single is not a default situation. Your life isn't a waiting game (you're not always "between relationships" when you're single). Not being in a relationship is a choice you make. *Own it.* And don't give it up so easily. "Don't wait for a man to buy you diamonds," says Hughes. "Buy that right hand ring! Do your own thing. Women need to think that the single time is the best time of your life. It's being able to be alone with yourself, reading a book. Being only responsible for you is such a wonderful sense of power—embrace that instead of worrying about it."

BOTTOM LINE

Think about everything you're giving up to be in a relationship. It's not worth the sacrifice if it's not the right guy. Yes, you need to know what you're looking for and not settle for less, but you don't need to find that on the first date. When I'm on a date, I don't worry whether he is going to be my future husband. And I know he's not the last man on earth. If it doesn't work out, I know that tomorrow—and well beyond—my life will go on. Always remember, that as a confident woman, you don't need to play games. Be happy with you and everything else will fall into place.

There's no excuse for feeling down about being on your own. I asked married and unmarried women to help me compile this list.

1. You have no responsibilities to anyone else but yourself.
2. You get to see your friends more often.
3. You shave your legs only when you feel like it.
4. You make all of your own plans.
5. You no longer "get in trouble."
6. The toilet seat is always down.
7. You don't have to watch your boyfriend play video games.
8. You don't have to suffer through his sports addictions.
9. You have the whole bed to yourself.
10. That all-consuming lust that you only experience at the beginning of a relationship.
11. The excitement of dressing up for first dates.
12. Watching whatever you want on TV.
13. Having the freedom to spend a Saturday doing whatever you want without having to explain yourself.
14. No mandatory dinners with your boyfriend's parents.

15. You can date lots of men, so you never get bored with just one.

16. "Going out" clothes actually have a purpose.

17. No one is going to look at your skirt and ask, "Don't you think that's a little too short?"

18. If you only want cereal for dinner, you can have it without needing to make a real meal for your husband.

19. You don't have to hide your purchases.

20. No one steals the blankets when you're asleep.

21. The feeling of independence.

22. No checking in.

23. No need to ask for approval or acceptance.

24. If someone finished the milk, you know it was you.

25. You can accept free drinks from men and not feel guilty about it.

26. The only morning breath you have to deal with is your own.

27. You don't have a condescending mother-in-law.

28. Your last name is still the one you had at birth.

29. The bathroom is all yours.

30. No stinky guy smells.

31. Chick flicks on Sunday afternoons.

32. When you have PMS, no one can tell you it's just an excuse to be bitchy.

33. You can stay in your pajamas all day and no one cares.

34. Friends can stop over anytime and you don't have to worry that someone else will be bothered.

35. The only things on TiVo are *Oprah, America's Next Top Model, Grey's Anatomy, Desperate Housewives,* and *What Not to Wear.* No *SportsCenter, Star Trek, Crocodile Hunter,* or *Baywatch.*

36. No one around to comment on the number of beauty products or shoes you own.

37. You still have an opportunity to hook up with Justin Timberlake if he suddenly knocked on your door.

38. You can turn on Britney Spears music and dance in front of the mirror and no one will walk in and make fun of you.

39. No one steals your shampoo.

40. The food in the fridge is all yours—which makes it easier to diet.

41. The alarm clock is set for when *you* need to wake up, not earlier.

42. No making conversation first thing in the morning.

43. No *Maxim* or *Stuff* magazines lying around.

44. The decor in your place reflects your taste; no ugly La-Z-Boy or old coffee table.

45. You can go to events with friends and not worry about your boyfriend fitting in.

46. All holidays are spent with your family.

47. No guys over for the big game.

48. No fighting for closet space.

49. You can change your hair and not have to consult with anyone.

50. The possibility of meeting someone special.

Part Two

The Forces of Evil

Chapter Four

Tell Mom—and Everyone Else— to %$#* Off

Dear [insert name],

I'm writing you this letter because there are a few things I want to tell you. I need you to listen, and I need you to listen carefully.

I know it's hard for you to accept that I am [insert age] and single—you certainly aren't shy about sharing this with me. However, instead of your criticism, I need your support and your acceptance.

Contrary to what you may believe, nothing is wrong with me. I am happy with who I am, and I am happy with my life. If I don't want to go on a date with someone who asks me out, it's okay. Please trust my judgment. I don't care that, if nothing else, "it's a free dinner." I can buy my own dinner.

I will not live a lonely, unhappy life just because I don't have a boyfriend at the moment. Although I don't have my own family yet, I have great friends who are like my family and give me much joy. I am single because I simply have the courage to wait for the right person. You should want that for me. I refuse to settle.

Love,

[your name]

P.S. Telling me I should be married will not make it happen sooner.

"At this point, all we need to find you is a man who can walk and who can breathe."

That's what 29-year-old Cindy's father said to her on a recent visit home. Anyone overhearing the conversation might have assumed Cindy, a teacher, was a lonely, desperate, insufferable, mean person who has never had a successful relationship. In fact, she is none of these things—she's just single.

Cindy has been with the same guy for a little more than two years. They're not engaged yet, but they've bought a condo together and marriage is definitely in the plans. She's been building a successful career, putting money in the bank, and enjoying her freedom so when the time comes to settle down, she'll be more than ready.

Sounds like Cindy has it all together, doesn't it? Well, her father obviously doesn't think so. He can't understand why she isn't married yet and constantly disparages her every time he sees her (which is no longer that often). A few more of his priceless comments:

"What are you waiting for? Don't you realize a person's worth is determined by his or her family?" (She basically

takes this to mean she's pretty worthless in his eyes because she doesn't have a family.)

"When you were six months old, I put money into an annuity to use for your wedding. It needs to be taken out after thirty years. Never in my life did I think you'd be single at 30 years old. I am now going to use the money to buy a BMW because a wedding is obviously not going to happen."

"Why do you keep dating men who won't marry you?" (Cindy is on her second long-term boyfriend over the last seven years; in other words, she's not bouncing from guy to guy.)

"Do you realize your eggs are rotting?" (My personal favorite.)

Correct me if I'm wrong, but aren't our parents supposed to love and comfort us and make us feel special, not like the biggest losers on the planet?

To varying degrees, we've all been in Cindy's shoes. I've had complete strangers approach me and tell me they worried that I was never going to be happy. *People who don't even know me, who've never even met the men I've dated.* I'm too polite to turn around and scream "F—k off!" but that's what I'm thinking. And I think the same thing when I hear stories from other women who are being tormented, insulted, and ridiculed for being single.

Thirty-year-old Detroit-based Andrea discovered her father's entire synagogue was concerned about her love life when the rabbi approached her at a party and announced, "We've been praying for you." A few months later, after Andrea had an unsuccessful blind date with a doctor, which had been arranged by her parents, Andrea's mother broke down on the phone. "You're going to live a lonely and depressed life!" she told her daughter through tears. Of course, that's not how Andrea saw it. She was disappointed, but she is confident she'll meet other men. Her parents, however, have written her off as an old maid. "I'd be lying if I said that my parents' lack of support hasn't deeply hurt me," she confesses.

At least her parents haven't gone to this extreme: posting a profile for her on an online dating site. Apparently, it's a new trend among desperate moms and dads. "Not too long ago," Lisa tells me, "my dad, whom I never discuss online dating with, cut out a newspaper article regarding Jdate.com and mothers posting profiles behind their children's backs. I told my mom that under no circumstance is she to do that. I would be so furious!" And she should be. The fun of online dating is being able to look for the kind of guy *you* like, based on *your* preferences—not your mother's. (As it is, 22 percent of Jdate.com's memberships are paid for by members' moms, according to a survey by the site.)

Even though women like Andrea and me are okay with being single, other people's angst does trigger moments of self-doubt. After all, when you're constantly being asked, "What's wrong with you?" (instead of "What's the matter with the guys you meet?") it's hard not to wonder if there really *is* something wrong. When a date doesn't work out, your parents should say, "That's all right. There will be others," not "Oh, no! You're going to be alone!" These people—often parents, sometimes friends—can make you feel so anxious that it's tempting to settle if only to shut them up. You think, Maybe they're right. Maybe *I'm* the one being ridiculous.

You're not. Sure, a lot of the time they have good intentions (even if they end up making you feel like a loser), and they want you to be happy. But often their idea of happy is different from yours. You know what's best for you. *You're* the one who is going to be in the relationship. Do not let anyone push you to accept less than you deserve.

"Years ago, I used to get pressure from my family," says Dawn. "But then my mother saw me traveling through Europe, renting a summer house, paying for a nice apartment and a car—and she started to see my friends get divorced—so she realizes my being single is a good thing and she's proud. She still wants love for me, but she's not pushing me at all."

Like Dawn, I'm lucky because my parents have never pressured me to get married. Still, my mother knows how much I'd like to be married one day, and I know she feels sorry for me. At times, I think she's more worried about me not walking down the aisle than I am. Like any good parent, she just wants my dream to come true. My mother is willing to wait for me to meet my soul mate because she trusts that I know what I'm doing. She believes in me.

Sometimes I wonder if my friends feel the same way. You'd assume, if anyone, they would understand my

life, but I've found they can be surprisingly condescending. One of my best friends, Carrie, is married to
a great guy and they have the cutest baby ever; they're
the perfect little family. One Friday night, I was hanging out in their apartment. Carrie was on the couch
with her baby on her lap and her husband by her side.
"What are you doing to meet someone?" she asked me.
"You're not going to meet someone by staying in with
us on a Friday night." I felt the sudden urge to leap
across the room and strangle her. Was she really saying
this to me?

NEWSFLASH . . . I know. We all know. I'm not *trying* to be single. Comments like Carrie's aren't motivat-
ing. They just make us feel bad about ourselves. It takes a
lot of energy to go out and meet people—and unless we
make it our full-time job, we can't do it 24/7. Not everyone is on the same schedule. Some parents and friends,
however, need a little convincing to comprehend that—
even tough love. Isn't that what they're giving *us*?

STAND UP FOR YOURSELF

Fighting with people about your social life isn't worth
the energy or the tears. You may not be able to change
their minds completely, but the goal is to get them to
understand your choices. "You have to make boundaries
in some way, shape, or form," advises psychotherapist
Dr. Jenn Berman. "To do that is to say, 'I'm really sorry
that you're having such a problem with my not having a

man in my life, but that's your issue. These are my feelings about it and I'm clear what your feelings are. It's all been said and we don't need to revisit it anymore unless something new comes up.'" Write them a letter (or just use the one at the beginning of this chapter). It will be much easier for you to get your feelings out when you're calm and they're not interrupting you. If your parents are worried because you don't have a man to support you, explain that this isn't the 1950s anymore and you're quite capable of supporting yourself. Women don't need a diamond ring to be complete (not that I don't occasionally find myself drooling over the massive rocks on the fingers of seemingly every woman I pass by—hey, I'm only human). Let them know their idea of happiness isn't yours. Tell them how fulfilled you are by having a great group of friends and a successful career. Tell them how amazing you really are. And if they keep demeaning you, cut off communication. Says relationship expert Dennie Hughes, "They will hear you if you come right out and say, 'I've already told you when you nag me, it bothers me. If you do this again, I will politely tell you good-bye and hang up or I won't come over again.'"

You can also throw some stats their way. Women who marry over age 30 only have about a 15 percent chance of getting divorced; for women five years younger, it's 25 percent. "It's funny when parents rush you to get married, and then they wonder 'What happened?' when you get divorced," says Hughes.

LESS IS MORE

Sometimes I'm afraid I tell my parents too much. I feel the need to warn 16-year-old girls to stop talking to their parents about their relationships. By the time you're 30, they will use everything they know against you— trust me on this. The more details you give them, the more questions they're going to ask. They're going to feel like they're entitled to discuss your personal life. If they know you're not dating, they'll worry and transfer that anxiety to you. You have to find the balance. If they're not good for your emotional well-being, limit your contact. Bully them like they bully you. If your parents ask you personal questions, inquire about their own romance. (Um, not that you necessarily want to know, but it will prove a point.)

CHOOSE YOUR MATCHMAKERS WISELY

Do not let your parents set you up. Whenever you let someone play matchmaker, you run the risk of disappointing that person if the date doesn't work out. It's hard enough to deal with it when the person is a friend or coworker, but it's infinitely worse when it's your parents (and they're dying for you to meet your soul mate). "The summer after my sophomore year in college, my mother answered a personal ad on my behalf," recalls Andrea. "I was mortified. My mom calmly explained that it was time for me to be in a serious relationship. Not surprisingly, the guy was a total loser. But sometimes I wish we had fallen in love and gotten married just so I wouldn't have had to put up with a decade's worth of nagging." No one can make you feel as guilty as your parents. Let them fix you up, and you're just begging for trouble. ("What are we going to tell his family?") They'll be too invested, ask too many questions, and, worst of all, may make you feel obligated to date a person you don't even like just to keep them quiet. It's not worth the drama.

GET SCRIPTED

"I always have to defend my single status to my father and other relatives," says magazine exec Sarah T., 30. Her solution? "I probably overcompensate by acting even busier and happier with my career, apartment, travel, and friends than I actually am. But I've also stopped apologizing for my relatives' confusion or disappointment. When my aunt Susan tells me, 'I don't understand, you're not dating that guy you were dating last time I saw you? I could have sworn . . .' I reply, 'Aunt Susan, I have no idea what or who you're talking about. I date lots of people, but no one remarkable, and I couldn't be happier."

Like Sarah, I'm always prepared for the inevitable questions about being single, and now I have comebacks ready to deliver.

Q: *"Why can't anyone see how great you are?"*
A: *"Maybe they* have *seen it, but I don't think they're so great."*

Q: *"All my friends ask me why you're not married yet."*
A: *"Tell them I haven't met the right guy. Would you prefer it if I was divorced now so you could at least say your daughter was once married?"*

Q: *"Why are you still single?"*
A: *"If I knew the answer to that question I wouldn't be single."* Duh. Or—*"Because I choose not to settle."*

Q: *How are you planning on getting out there and meeting someone?*
A: *"I plan on living my life and I know that someone will eventually come along."*

IF THE TRUTH HURTS . . .

Sometimes, the only way to get people to stop badgering you about being single is to flat out lie. (How many movies have been made in which a woman hires a man to be her date? And they usually fall in love.) No, it's not the most ethical thing to do, but if it preserves your sanity—and keeps you from settling—by all means go for it. Whatever it takes for you to be okay with you, short of hurting other people. Tell your parents you're dating someone but you're superstitious and you don't want to jinx it. If they demand a name, be sure to give them one that is Google-proof—either too random to turn up anything, or so common that they'll be overwhelmed with results. In a few weeks, tell them you were dumped. Let them think you're heartbroken. Tell them you need some time to heal and that you don't trust men anymore. You'll buy yourself a few months of peace and quiet.

BOTTOM LINE

Take control. Stand up to the people who constantly put pressure on you to be in a relationship. They can make you feel so anxious that it can be tempting to settle just to make them stop. Whether you're single or married is your decision only—nobody else's. You have control over how you feel. Remind yourself every day that you are fabulous just the way you are. Do not let anyone bring you down or make you think something's wrong with you. Don't let them make you feel like your expectations are too high. Trust your gut.

Chapter Five

"But All My Friends Are Married . . ."

W hen banker Joanie was 32 years old, *she felt as if all of her girlfriends—"from college, from work, from everywhere"—were getting hitched. "I was dating my boyfriend for five years, and I saw friends who had been dating for a much shorter period of time getting engaged and married. I wasn't going to be the loser without a husband," she says. So when her boyfriend proposed—something they had never even discussed—she went along with it. "In my mind, my best dating years were behind me. I was going to get a return on this time investment!" Her wedding day wasn't one of those magical moments. "I walked down the aisle knowing I was doing the wrong thing, but dammit, I was going to get married no matter what." Now 45 and divorced, she tells me getting married "was the worst mistake of my life."*

Last Woman Standing. It's not a title anyone strives to achieve, but inevitably, there's a woman in every group of friends who earns it. Instead of a crown and a tiara, the winner often walks away with a (seemingly) endless supply of self-doubt, feelings of being left behind, and an evil little voice inside her head screaming, "Just find someone—*anyone*—and catch up!"

I am an LWS, but I choose not to accept any of the prizes that come with the title. My friends, most of whom are in long-term relationships, used to joke that they'd be on their third husbands while I'd still be single. It's not as if I always planned to be everyone's "plus one," but here I am. As much as I would like to be paired off, I would never start a relationship just because everyone else is doing it.

Married New Hampshire–based publicist Sarah L., 32, recalls, "When I was 26, I was ready to move on to the next stage in life. I didn't feel pressure from anyone else saying I should be married, but I saw all of my friends doing it and I thought, I want that." Similarly, Cleveland-based Katie, 26, says her yearning to be in a relationship comes from "everyone around me finding the 'right' person and getting married. My closest friends from high school and college are married, and everyone in my department at work is married. A few years ago we had a holiday party with spouses, and of fifty people I was the *only one* without a date. Thankfully, I bring enough fun with me for two people, so it's not a big deal. But still . . ."

Marital clocks tick louder when friends start having kids and you're still trying to find a boyfriend. I remember when my friend Lauren had a baby. I thought, How can she be a mom when it seems as if we're still in college? I don't feel ready to have a child. How can she? It can be unsettling, and you just wonder when it's going to be your turn. Single Blair, who didn't date anyone seriously for her first ten years out of college, says, "I have friends who have two kids already, and other friends whose first marriages are already over." She only has two single friends left—and one is divorced. "I feel like people are lapping me. It's not like I want to sprint to catch up. It's more like I want to yell, 'Hey, slow down!'"

Love is not a competition. Having married friends is not a valid reason to get married. A relationship is about two people, not your five closest pals and their husbands. Of course there are times when I wonder if I *ever* will find someone to marry, but when I hear a story like Joanie's, I know I'm doing the right thing by not jumping the gun.

ABOUT PACE

When it seems like everyone but me is on the path to "I do," I ease the pressure I feel by doing a few things: First, I take a deep breath and tell myself that my time will come. You have to believe that if you don't want to settle. Then, I think about the fact that 46 percent of American women are also unmarried. Finally, I remind myself that everybody's life happens at a different pace. Sure, most people hit certain milestones at around the same time—orthodontia, graduations—but to compare yourself to other people just doesn't make sense. We don't all get promotions at the same time. We all don't buy homes at the same time. And there is no set schedule for falling in love.

Nevertheless, marriage is something we're all trained to think about, and plan on, from an early age. It's deemed the ultimate goal in life. Girls talk about their wedding day, their dress, and who will be their bridesmaids before they even hit 18. Once adulthood arrives, the fixation intensifies: My friend Megan, 30, is obsessed with weddings and diamond rings. She's even hung a picture of her favorite gem on her refrigerator door. She doesn't have any idea when she's getting married, but she wants to be prepared when her time comes.

For an LWS, diamonds can be inspiring—"I can't wait until I meet the right guy and get an amazing ring," many women will say—but they can also be evil. Patty once shared an office with five women, all of whom had serious boyfriends. "During our downtime, we'd look at rings on the Internet," she recalls. "At lunch, we'd make scouting trips to Tiffany and Co." One by one, they got engaged—except for her coworker Elena, whose boyfriend was taking his time proposing. "She became really anxious and depressed," says Patty. "I'm sure if she was in an office filled with single people she would have been fine, but it was really in her face. It wasn't even that

Elena and Mitch had such a great relationship—in fact, they eventually broke up—but she just wanted to be able to compare rings with everyone else and feel like part of the group."

If you focus too much attention on the idea of getting a ring or having a wedding, you'll lose sight of the most important thing: the *marriage*. When I walk down the aisle, I want to feel 100 percent certain that the man waiting at the altar is the best person for me. I won't let the glare of a diamond cloud my judgment. In fact, I've had one, and I assure you it doesn't guarantee happiness.

GUEST RELATIONS

Forget worrying about your own wedding; for an LWS, making it through other people's nuptials can be a challenge. If you're depressed about being single, all weddings seem to do is slap you in the face. I've noticed that the more weddings I attend (I've had a steady flow since I was 22), the smaller the singles table gets. At a certain point, it no longer becomes the place to be. Instead, it feels like you're seated all alone in loser central and all you want to do is sit with the cool kids—all of whom have dates. "For a year and a half after my divorce was finalized, I had one wedding each month," recalls Valerie. "At my cousin's wedding, I was seated at a table with my grandparents, her in-laws, and one elderly gentleman." After every wedding, you make a note to self: Find a boyfriend in time for the next one. "I just realized I have to be really drunk to deal with being by myself at a wedding," moaned single writer Andrea in a phone call made during the middle of a reception. She added, "I can't even show my folks the photos from my friends' weddings because I see the looks on their faces and know what they're thinking." By Andrea's estimate, once she actually finds a date to bring to a wedding, all of her friends will be married. "It won't even matter anymore!"

I don't particularly enjoy being among the single minority at a wedding, but I don't let it ruin my night, either. I see the romance in a hopeful light, not as something meant to torture me. If you sit around sulking in the corner wondering why you're not the one cutting the cake, you prove the stereotype that single woman are pathetic. Stand tall, grab a cocktail, and strut your stuff around the party. Show the world that you're okay being on your own. The worst thing you can do is be the pathetic wallflower. When you send off a positive vibe and demonstrate that you're having fun, you never know what might happen: "I was on the buffet line at a friend's wedding and a woman I didn't even know approached me and asked if I was single," recalls Blair. "She ended up fixing me up with her nephew."

Dr. Debbie Then says it's never a good idea to bring a date just to have a date. She explains, "You won't be mingling or meeting other people."

ALL BY MYSELF

Weddings aren't the only time singles can feel especially left out. When my friends have couples nights, they often just assume I wouldn't want to be included. But I'm not going to start dating someone just so I can have my own Pictionary team. Besides, there's no way my friends would want me to bring some loser into the mix. Still, it does piss me off that certain people only want to make plans when I'm in a relationship. One of my friends— who shall remain nameless—only sees me during the afternoon when I'm single; every time I have a boyfriend, she wants to schedule something for a Friday or Saturday night. "Come over," she'll say. "I'll make dinner, we'll have wine. It'll be fun!" Why can't I be invited over on a weekend evening on account of being me, and not *only* when I'm part of a couple?

Not many LWSs will admit this, but I know many of them have a secret fantasy that all of their coupled friends will break up so they can go back to the way it used to be when they were all single and carefree. Cara, a 30-year-old public relations manager confesses, "Sometimes, when a friend gets dumped, I'm secretly glad. I hate to admit it and I know that probably makes me sound horrible. It's just nice to feel like I haven't been abandoned." I can understand how she feels. I don't want my friends to be miserable, lonely, or sad, but it's nice to have someone who gets what I'm going through.

New Yorker Catherine R. says she isn't lacking

friends, but grumbles, "The ones who are most similar to me are married. Now I feel like I don't have a group of girls who want to go where I would go to possibly meet men. I feel somewhat limited. I don't want to go to a dingy dive bar where everyone is 25."

When your single friends do get into relationships, it's bittersweet. "I have one close friend who just found a great boyfriend," Katie tells me. "I am so happy for her, but it just reminds me that I want to find someone, too. No matter how much fun you have, no matter how fabulous it is to be independent and answer to no one, deep down you can't help wanting to find the right person to spend your life with. I can totally understand why on *Friends,* Rachel slept with Ross the night their pals Monica and Chandler announced their engagement."

Many of the women I interviewed say online dating sites—of which there are over 1,000—are a great place to turn when all of your friends have paired off. (I confess: I'm afraid to try it—even though I know it seems like a better idea than looking for love on TV.) "Online dating was helpful just to show me how many people are out there when you feel like you have dated everyone on the planet and there is no one left," says married L.A.-based entrepreneur Annalise, 34. "I had several friends meet their future husbands and wives online, so that was encouraging, too." Heather also finds it fits in better with her busy lifestyle. "I spend so much time in the office," she says, "I just don't have the free time to go out and meet people. I also think it's good for people over 30 who are not into the bar scene." Fans of online dating offer so many reasons why they love it, but Rachel's is my favorite: "It's like shopping for boys—and you can do it in your pajamas while watching TV."

Here's the thing: If you do feel left out because all of your girlfriends are married (or in relationships), the solution is not to run out and find yourself a *boy*friend. Think about all of the other single women in this country. You're bound to be able to make a connection with at least one or two. "I met one of my best friends at a neighborhood teahouse," recalls Rebecca. "All of these interesting people—totally different, all single—would hang out there, and they formed their own community." I've made friends with my kickboxing instructor and several people in my office. Always knowing that I have the ability to adapt and make friends in any situation is comforting. This way, even when I'm single, I don't have to be alone.

THIRD-WHEEL SYNDROME

For me, one of the worst things about being an LWS is that even when your attached friends *do* include you in social activities—as they should—you still stick out. At dinners, I always feel weird when my odd chair is squeezed onto the end of a table for four. Or when it's time to pay the bill, someone is stuck doing long division to figure out how much *I* owe. If that's too hard (or they're just generous) they might end up paying for me, which leads to feelings of guilt. I always wonder, do they feel sorry for me? Do they think I came out for the free meal? Do I have to take them out to dinner next? (If that's the case, I try not to plan that dinner around the holidays, when my girlfriends talk about the jewels they received as presents and I have to brag about pajamas from my mom.) "Before I got married, I tried to spend time with my friends who were in relationships," says recruiter Amy, 31. "But I definitely balanced it by spending time with my single friends or on my own so I didn't feel like an out-of-place reject."

Dinners are easy compared to going on vacations with your attached friends. Shannon is currently caught in a typical single woman's dilemma: She was the only single person among her friends who was invited to a wedding in London. "A lot of the people who are going are staying on to make a trip to Ireland," she explains. "But it's all couples. I've already been to Ireland and done that trip, so I don't want to go. But at the same time, I also don't want to go because I don't want to be the ninth wheel. I've known these people for years and I love the husbands as much as the wives, but I would feel awkward going back to my hotel room at night alone." The good news is she's not going to let her lack of a date ruin a great opportunity. "Maybe I'll go to Paris with another single friend," she says.

I had a similar predicament last summer: My friend planned a trip to Napa for her 30th birthday, and she invited several couples—and me, by myself—to join in the celebration. I was afraid the trip would be a romantic getaway for everyone else, but I didn't want to miss out on the fun or disappoint my friend. I considered bringing my brother, but then I realized I didn't need him as a wingman. I plan to go and have fun with the group.

The trick to surviving these situations is to change your perspective. Don't look at these third- (or ninth-) wheel situations as a bunch of couples plus you. See the group as a whole. It's an odd number of people who happen to be men and women (and some of them live together), but *it's just a group*. Besides, when couples socialize, the women tend to huddle in one corner while the men talk in another. Clearly, your friends don't have a problem with you being a party of one, so why should you? Stop worrying and enjoy yourself. It's definitely a better way to spend your time than sitting at home feeling pitiful. (Especially because you know you're not.)

THE GRASS IS ALWAYS GREENER . . .

The more you tag along with couples, the more you'll realize their lives aren't perfect. Says divorced sales rep Ashley, "I always go on dates with my friends and their husbands or boyfriends, as a third wheel. Sometimes it makes me really sad and lonely, sometimes it makes me appreciate how much I've grown, and sometimes it makes me glad that I am not in a relationship like theirs."

I don't believe any of my friends in relationships are

happier than I am. In fact, one long-term study conducted by a professor at Michigan State University found that two years into marriage, couples rated their happiness at the exact same level as they did before they wed. And I don't need a researcher to tell me that people in relationships are often envious of the single life. When my friend Carrie wakes up on Saturday mornings at 5:30 A.M. to tend to her baby, she wishes she could trade places with me. When I go out with my other girlfriends, she wants to know all the details. "What did you wear? Where did you go? What did you eat?" I'm sure she's jealous that the only mess I have to clean up is my own. And then there's my mother's friend Sue, 52, who loves her husband dearly, but once told me that if anything ever happened to him, she'd date but she'd never live with another man again—it's just too annoying.

BOTTOM LINE

If you're putting pressure on yourself to be in a relationship, think about how often your pals come to you to complain about their boyfriends, husbands, and kids. I see my friends fight about money (which I know a lot of people do), their friends, time spent at work, and so on. I see them not communicating. I lend an ear when they complain about their in-laws.

Do I want to deal with all of those issues? Only if I'm with the right person.

Chapter Six

Stop Believing You Can't Do Better

Jenny and Tom, both 30, are college sweethearts who have been married for eight years. After their wedding, Jenny breathed a sigh of relief because she thought she had it all: a perfect little marriage to the cutest guy in the Delta Tau Delta house. What she didn't anticipate was how much they were both going to change over the next few years. The gregarious fraternity boy has become a serious man, a banker who spends little time at home. Meanwhile, Jenny, who has spent the last eight years working on her career in pharmaceutical sales, has decided she wants to put off having children—leaving Tom confused. Hadn't they decided years ago (probably when they were both about 18) that they were going to have kids? They've completely grown apart. The passion they once had for each other is gone. Not only does Jenny not love Tom anymore, she doesn't even like him. I asked her once why she doesn't leave and she said, "I can't. I've been with him forever. Who else would put up with my quirks? I can be moody and messy and *spend too much money sometimes. What if he's the only person who can deal with me? Maybe I'm crazy, but I'm afraid if I let him go, I'm going to be 60 and look back and think I gave up the love of my life."*

There's nothing sadder than a woman who sells herself short in a relationship, whether we're talking about an eight-year marriage or an eight-week fling. You should never stick with someone you aren't 100 percent sure about just because you're afraid you won't do any better. If you're a self-assured woman with a lot to offer, there's no excuse for it. "Life is just way too fun to be stuck in some relationship that isn't really all that satisfying," notes single Melissa.

Low self-esteem is another one of the forces of evil that drives women to settle. It leads us to think a bad relationship is as good as it gets, even when what we have isn't any good at all. Jenny doesn't believe anyone else will love her but Tom. (By the way, if "quirks" such as PMS and a shopping habit are so repellant, then we're all in trouble.) She thinks she's peaked when, in fact, Tom is the only guy she's been with since her freshman year in college. Instead of seeking the happiness they truly deserve, women like Jenny are resigned to be unfulfilled. As ivillage.com dating expert Sherry Amatenstein explains, "To some women, the known hell is preferable to the unknown."

I don't get it. And I certainly know all about the concept of thinking you can't do better. Many people thought I had the ultimate catch in Andrew Firestone, and when we broke up, they reminded me every day how I was never going to find another guy like him. Did I believe it? Yes, but not for reasons that you might think. Without a doubt, he is a fabulous catch and I am not going to do better. But it's not about finding someone better than Andrew Firestone. It's about finding someone who better *for me*. Let me explain: If you're basing your judgment solely on a person's pedigree, then yes, it's safe to say I probably will not find another nice-looking heir to a tire fortune winemaker. However, his physical appearance and occupation were not the issue. Our personalities were too different to have a successful relationship. While I think he's a great guy, I was unhappy dating him. I had to separate myself from all of those much-desired qualities and think about what was ultimately going to make me happy. I'm not trying to trade up for more money, status, or looks; my motivation isn't superficial. I'm trading up for happiness. At the time Andrew and I broke up, I believed—and still do—that there is someone more perfect for me (and him, for that matter) out there in the world. For that reason alone, I *know* I'm going to do better. Maybe not on paper, but where it matters most: in my heart.

DON'T BE A DOORMAT

If a man isn't giving you what you need and making you feel good about yourself, you owe it to yourself to move on. I once had a boyfriend—I'll call him Cocky Bastard—who loved to remind me how lucky I was to be in his company. C.B. was good-looking, successful, incredibly well-liked (by those who didn't know him well), and pretty much could have dated any woman he wanted. It's no wonder I fell for him initially. As we began dating, though, I realized he didn't treat me all that well, and I voiced my unhappiness. He honestly said to me, "Do you know how many girls would kill to be in the situation you're in with me?" I did. Even though I wasn't lacking in self-esteem, I still questioned myself. A lot of women *would* have loved to be with him (in theory). Should I just be glad to be in this relationship? Am I expecting too much? At the time, I stayed with him because as much as that comment angered me, I thought he was right. But that didn't make it okay for me to put up with his inability to think about anyone but himself. Eventually, I called it quits. I knew I couldn't let him (or even that annoying voice inside my head) convince me that unhappiness is an ideal state of being. I've yet to meet the man of my dreams, but I've never had any regrets that C.B. and I broke up—despite what he might think.

There are so many men like C.B. out there. Boston-based project administrator Clare, 23, put up with one for six months. "He would be wonderful, and then a bit of a jerk, and then wonderful again," she recalls. "I convinced myself—with his help, of course—that I was actually the one making him say awful things to me, and that he was, in fact, a really nice guy who was putting up with my annoyingness." Finally she woke up to his behavior (and her own) and decided she'd had enough. "I realized how awful he made me feel, and that nothing I was doing actually warranted his behavior," she explains. "Gotta love those moments of clarity."

Observing other people's relationships is what prompted business analyst Annie to raise her standards. "I saw my girlfriends date normal guys and thought, Why is my boyfriend cheap, lazy, and rude? It takes awhile to stand up for yourself and realize you deserve more. But the more you see, the more you realize what's possible. With age, we wise up and recognize we're better off taking care of one person—yourself—rather than two."

Political consultant Carly, 28, who stayed in a boring ("That's as high as my expectations were," she confesses) relationship for three and a half years, says men can be just as much to blame as we are in these circumstances. "They are secretly insecure and a little bit lazy," she says. "There's an 'if it ain't broke' mentality that can be explained as 'I can't do better,' but I think it means 'I'm not willing to do better.'"

SPARE TACTICS

Seeking out the best situation doesn't mean hopping from guy to guy. (If you've read chapter 1, you'll know why.) As hard as it may be, simply leaving the bad relationship is all it takes. You don't need a one-upper waiting in the wings. New Yorker Sarah T. acknowledges there have been times where she didn't think she could do better. "Coming to grips with the idea that being alone might constitute 'doing better' was a very difficult process. But as it turns out, I could and I did."

My friend Bridget, 29, hasn't reached that stage yet. In fact, she's currently torn between two men: her official boyfriend, Paul, and her man on the side, Alan. She wants to be with Alan, but he doesn't want a serious relationship with her. So in the meantime, she's sticking it out with Paul even though she isn't in love with him anymore. Her rationale? She doesn't want to be alone and miss out on marriage and having a baby. Basically, she's keeping him on the back burner because she fears he may be her only hope. When we (her friends) tell her to break up with Paul she replies, "What if Alan doesn't want me and then I never meet anyone again?" It makes me sad to hear her say this. I'd do anything to get her to feel differently.

Everyone experiences those "what if" moments at some time or another. I do it all the time when I think about old boyfriends. Sometimes, to knock some sense into myself, I literally have to write down all the guy's bad traits and all of the reasons why the relationship didn't work. I also bring out old e-mails I've kept that contain disagreements. I reread them and realize how exhausting the relationship became; it puts everything back into perspective.

Relationship expert Dennie Hughes suggests a similar strategy to use when you're questioning your relationship. "Write a letter to yourself about all the things that are bad within your relationship. Instead of signing it from yourself, sign it as someone important to you, like your mother or best friend. Then, reread the letter as if it's coming from that person. Most people agree they would never want their loved one to be in a relationship like this. Love *yourself* that much and get out of it."

INFINITE (OR CLOSE TO IT) POSSIBILITIES

There are approximately forty million single men in the United States alone. No, you're not going to meet all of them. It also doesn't mean the next guy, or even the next ten guys, will be better than the last. But it only takes one, and I'll never run out of possibilities. I've seen what happens to people who give up hope: My friend Lindsay's parents got married when they were 28—in those days, that was considered old. Her mom was an LWS. They never really loved each other, but they felt like they had run out of options and just needed to wed in order to have children. Now, they are so miserable with each other and with their lives. I don't think I've ever heard them say a kind word to each other. They stayed together only for the kids, but the kids would like nothing more than for their parents to end the marriage, end their misery, and find happiness elsewhere.

According to a 1996 U.S. Census stat—that was the last time this calculation was made—if you were single at 40, you still had a 40.8 percent chance of getting married someday. Those are encouraging odds. As long as I continue to believe the right man is somewhere in this *universe,* I won't settle for anything less.

Dr. Jenn Berman says fear of male scarcity is one of the top reasons women stay in bad relationships. "The mentality is that there aren't enough men available in the world so I might as well put up with this crappy guy instead of actually taking a risk and going out there and seeing what's out there." People also avoid breakups, she says, because they're hoping that the relationship will return to the initial honeymoon phase. "Most relationships go through a really good stage before they go bad. We tend to hold on to that and say, If only I do x, y, and z I can figure out how to make things good again." Another rationale for why women put up with being miserable is because they don't believe in themselves. "They don't have the confidence that they will be okay on their own," she says, "or that they will be able to find someone who will make them happier." Hughes offers one additional explanation: "Some of these people are people pleasers and they only stay because everyone else is thrilled with the guy." (More on this in chapter 8.)

Regardless of the motivation, staying in a bad relationship can wreak havoc on your sense of worth. "It erodes your self-esteem," says Berman. That, in turn, doesn't bode well for your future. She explains, "You're less likely to find someone when you have low self-esteem."

NO END IN SIGHT

No matter how down you're feeling, you can't forget that it is possible to fall in love with more than one person in your lifetime—and more than one person will love you. New chances come along all the time. "Every time love has kicked me in the ass it's when I least expected it," says Amy. "I was always in a party or selfish mode, not wanting that part of my life to change or stop and then WHAM! Some dude that I don't really think much about at first comes barreling into my life."

Each time one of my relationships fizzles, I think, Oh no, here I go once more. How am I *ever* going to meet anyone again? And then another guy pops up. I know that the love I've experienced so far hasn't been the type I feel I need to devote my life to a person, but I believe the best is yet to come. Women like Jennifer Aniston and Nicole Kidman inspire me. Most people would agree you can't top Brad Pitt or Tom Cruise (back in his pre-couch-jumping days), however, it sure looks as if they've been willing to try.

People get second chances at love all of the time. Had Carly stayed in her ho-hum relationship with her college boyfriend—and married him—she never would have met Charlie and actually learned what it's like to be excited about growing old with someone. "I didn't think you could have passion with someone who is good for you," she says. "I was wrong." After unsuccessful attempts to convince a former boyfriend that they shouldn't break up, Rebecca tried to bounce back by posting her photo on an online dating site. "I was looking to feel better and get some validation," she says. "I ended up meeting my husband."

Even after a broken engagement and a failed marriage, Valerie still believes in love. "Since my divorce three years ago, I've been nothing but hurt by men," she says. "My friends say every time it happens, I think it's the last guy on earth who I think is going to care about me. The reality is, they just keep getting better."

BOTTOM LINE

Never give up. The only time you're allowed to say you don't think you can do better? When he's perfect for you and you can't imagine being with anyone else.

Chapter Seven

. . . .

Triantapentephobia

T ri an ta pen ta pho bia n. 1. An abnormal fear of the number 35, common among single women and related to the age when experts say fertility begins to significantly decline. 2. A force of evil that makes many women settle.

Example: "Seeing five close friends have babies in the last year has really made me worry about my biological clock," says single business analyst Annie, 28. "It's also led me to think I should shut up and get married already. I wouldn't have given a passing thought to any of it five years ago, but I definitely do now. I really hadn't thought about marriage much before I thought about babies."

Forget 13; for single women with dreams of motherhood, 35 is the scariest number. We've all heard the statistic that a woman's fertility drops 50 percent at that age (I won't even share the grimmer truth about what happens in your forties), and there's nothing anyone can do to change that. "It's not so much a matter of difficulty getting pregnant," explains my gynecologist, Dr. Abbie Roth, a clinical instructor at Northwestern Memorial Hospital in Chicago, "but the fragility of the DNA starts to increase." As much as we say we want to hold out for Mr. Right, our bodies are operating on their own timetables.

Here's my quandary: I am 30 years old. I want to date someone for at least a year, possibly two, before getting engaged. I expect the engagement period will last at least another twelve months. Then, I want to be married for at least two years before I start trying for a baby—which places me in the delivery room somewhere around the age of 34 or 35. In other words, if I want to stay ahead of the fertility game, I pretty much have to meet my future husband . . . yesterday.

I'm not going to panic.

If I turn into a desperate woman, I'll just end up repelling men instead of attracting them. (*Bachelor* fans will remember 33-year-old Allie from Travis Stork's show—the woman who told him she was ready to "reproduce" and later discussed her "rotting" eggs with the other women. She couldn't understand why she didn't receive a rose.) As much as I would love to be a mom, I'm not about to throw my needs out the door to make that dream come true. The worst thing you could do for yourself (not to mention your future offspring) is rush into a relationship and settle for a person who is just "good enough." I don't want my husband to be a virtual sperm donor; I want him to be someone I can't live without. If 35 comes and goes and I'm still unmarried, it's not the end of the world: Twenty percent of American women have their first child after 35, and the birth-rate keeps rising.

THE ONSET OF SYMPTOMS

Cases of triantapentaphobia vary in degrees of serious-ness, but three things tend to aggravate it: alarming news headlines ("Fading Fertility Hits Women in Their 20s" announced one BBC News story on the Internet), alarm-ist family members, and friends with children (i.e., "But all my friends have babies . . ."). Fortunately, only one of my closest friends is a mom, so I'm not *constantly* re-minded that I'm nowhere near starting a family of my own. In fact, after taking care of her 19-month-old son while she was out of town for two days, I'm more than happy to wait a while longer. Single life is much more exciting than entertaining a toddler.

My triantapentaphobia first hit me when I was 28, not long after I broke up with my last serious boyfriend and realized I had no prospects on the horizon. Even though your twenties are supposed to be a carefree time, it's hard not to fret about the future. "I am 26 and totally *not* ready for kids," says Katie. "But I worry that I'll get to a point where I have to decide to not have kids or have them on my own. Everyone says, 'Oh, you'll get married someday,' but that's easy for them to say when they are already married. There are no guarantees! I can't wait and count on something that could never happen." Twenty-five-year-old Natalie, a Columbus, Ohio–based high school teacher, says she, too, is already "a little bit" worried about her biological clock. "Most of that comes with the thought that I don't want to be 70 at my child's high school graduation," she says. One of her friends is much more afflicted. "She is 27 and single. She is so worried about her biological clock that she wants to be artificially inseminated at age 32! I'm making it my personal goal to talk her out of it."

In your early thirties, the internal panic combines with external pressure, and your anxiety will intensify if you don't keep a level head. "People ask me all the time, 'Don't you want to have kids?'" says Shannon, 33. "Yes! More than anything. Just because I'm not married doesn't mean I can't have kids. That question bothers me a lot." It also doesn't help that some of her male friends make disparaging comments about single women of a certain age. "They all say things like, 'Women over 35 who aren't married are crazy. They must have something wrong with them or have issues.' To hear that from these guys whom I like and respect, and who respect me, is awful."

Men who say things like that are imbeciles, and they only prove why it's difficult to meet a great guy. You can't let absurd and offensive comments like that get to you: If you settle, the assholes win.

At 38, Dawn has managed to keep her triantapenta-phobia in check with a combination of confidence and hopefulness. "If I wanted to lobotomize myself, I could be pregnant and married," she says. "But I at least want to go in to a marriage with my best foot forward." Even though she admits, "I do get a little sad occasionally because I'd love to be a mom," she isn't caving. "Whatever is going to be is going to be. I'm not going to try and make something wrong work for the sake of having a baby."

And how does a single woman in her forties cope? By expanding her dating pool. "While I have worked through the possibility that I may never have my own biological children, I love kids and would love someone else's too," explains Heather. "So, with a great deal of support from my shrink, Dr. B., I decided that dating men with kids was a viable option. It has taken the pressure off."

FAMILY BUSINESS

When you start to worry about your future as a mother, ask yourself this question: Do you want to be in a marriage and raise kids with someone you really don't love? Although children bond people together, they can also tear them apart. Parenting is a huge challenge, and if you're not a team, your relationship will suffer. My friend Lindsay's mom (the unhappy one) is constantly reminding her, "Don't get married just to have kids!"

Joanie, another former LWS, actually missed out on her chance to have kids *because* she settled. "I knew deep in my heart that my husband would make a lousy father," she explains, "and I'd also be saddled with his hideous family for the rest of my life. So, despite his mom's constant barrage of ugly criticism about my lack of motherhood, I refused to let myself get pregnant." Now divorced and childless at 45, she acknowledges, "Perhaps, if I'd waited, I would have found someone who would have been a better dad. Or, perhaps, I'd have been in a more stable place to be a single mother." Either way, she says, "I think it's better to take your chances and possibly remain unmarried. If you don't settle, you will be better off in the long run."

AGE-OLD ISSUES

Even though we can't change how our bodies work, we don't have to freak out about it. One thing that calms me down is seeing so many women having kids in their forties: Madonna had Rocco when she was 43; Geena Davis gave birth to twins at 48. The oldest woman to ever give birth was 66. (It's safe to assume she did not use her own eggs—neither do most moms over 45.) I hope I don't have to wait that long, but at least I know that if I'm not married by the time I'm 35, it doesn't mean I can never have a baby.

Valerie, 32, often worries she gave up her chance to become a mom when she got divorced, but recently received some heartening news from her ob-gyn during her annual checkup. "I was having a very dark day," she says. "So I asked him, 'Am I okay to have children?' And he said, 'My God, you're so young. The average age of women have babies in my practice is 38. Enjoy yourself. Have fun because once you have kids, they don't go away.'" Valerie began to cry. "Having a baby is so important to me," she says. "He gave me hope that there was time."

And, of course, there's also science. According to Joseph C. Isaacs, president and CEO of RESOLVE: The National Infertility Association, with proper and timely medical attention, infertility treatments have a 70 to 80 percent success rate. "This is a condition that can be remedied," he says. Options include in vitro fertilization, surrogacy, and egg, sperm, or embryo donation. (Egg freezing—which could be considered the equivalent of hitting the snooze bar on your biological clock—is available at some fertility clinics, but many experts warn that it is highly unreliable and still experimental.) Of course, none of these are simple procedures, and infertility itself can cause a woman (and a man) a lot of physical and emotional stress. It's another reason not to settle: If you're going to go through all of that, you want to make sure you're doing it with the right person by your side. "Having emotional support is key to all of this," stresses Isaacs.

BACKUP PLANS
. . . .

Like all single women, I've spent a lot of time wondering about my future and specifically what I would do if I were still on my own ten years from now. What would be my Plan B? Settling would never be an option, but I would definitely consider having a baby on my own. While unmarried mothers used to be ostracized or pitied, today, it's not unusual for a woman in her thirties or forties to hit the sperm bank (in 2005, one-third of the clients at the California Cryobank—the country's largest depository—were single women), contact an adoption agency, or get help (i.e., DNA) from a male friend in order to have the baby of her dreams. According to the National Center for Health Statistics, in 2004, 35.7 percent of all births were to unmarried women—up 3 percent from the previous year. (There's even an organization called Single Mothers by Choice.)

If I hit 38 and I have no prospects, I would seriously start to weigh my options. Ultimately, I'd like to have a baby with my own DNA, but I'd definitely consider adoption. When I told that to my mom and dad, their (typical parent) reaction was, "You won't need to." Maybe that's true, but I might as well start preparing them for anything at this point.

I know my parents would like to see me get married before I become a mom, but some parents reach a point where they're more interested in having a grandchild

than a son-in-law. "One Thanksgiving," recalls Melanie, "as my immediate family was discussing my single
status (again), my mother said, 'You know, I really think
you have to be a mom. You'll be such a good mom. So
even if you never get married, I think you should consider artificial insemination. I would support you!'"

Marketing and publicity director Candice's mother,
on the other hand, thought her single daughter was "giving up" when, at 35, she decided to pursue adoption.
Candice had been engaged in her twenties, and a few
serious relationships followed, but she never felt the desire to marry. "I knew I always wanted to be a mom, but
not a wife," she explains. "In my early thirties, I decided
if I get to 35 and I'm not married, I don't want to spend
my life worrying if I'll have kids or not. The closer I got
to 35, the closer I came to wanting it." She began the
adoption process at 36, but quickly realized she wasn't
ready—especially because she wanted her mother's support. When her mom came finally around, Candice
consulted with a financial adviser to make sure she could
care for a child, and then began the process of adopting
a baby girl from China. With her daughter's arrival only
a few months away, Candice, now 38, tells me, "The
thought of being a single mother is scary, but not scary.
I have married friends who complain and tell me their
husbands are useless. Hearing that, I know I'd rather be
doing it by myself."

Another woman who didn't let singleness stop her
from becoming a mom is Pam, a photographer and

mother to an adopted 18-month-old girl. Four years ago, when she was 39 and still single, she had a reality check. "The thought of getting married and having a biological child started to seem more unlikely," she explains. "But I have always been quite independent in my life, so being single wasn't this huge heartbreaking thing. It was more like, okay, whatever with the husband and the marriage—how am I going to have a baby?" After unsuccessful attempts to get pregnant with help from a gay friend, and then with an on-again-off-again boyfriend, Pam realized the best bet was adoption. "A couple close friends of mine had adopted, plus, my circle of friends is very accepting of alternative lifestyles, so there was never a moment when I wondered if it would raise any eyebrows." Pam shared the same fears as Candice ("Can I do it on my own? Will I be a good mom?"), but says her daughter has been well worth it. "The payoff for tackling the fear and rising to the challenge of being a single mom is that there is nothing as special and unique and fulfilling as the love you have for your kid," she says. "Nothing. It is the most gratifying emotion I have experienced."

These women are such amazing role models. They give me hope and ease my anxiety that I have to be married and have kids by 35. And it's not as if they've sworn off men, either. They still dream that one day they'll find lasting love. But for now, Candice says, "Thank God I'm not in a marriage where I'm arguing with someone about how to raise my child, or them not helping. If you're going to be in a marriage and you've waited a long time, you might as well have all the things you waited for."

BOTTOM LINE

You don't have to put a deadline on yourself and your relationship status. Yes, 35 is a significant age fertility-wise, but it's no reason to lower your standards, sell yourself short, or give in to panic just to be with a man. Many women have babies into their forties. It might be harder, but it's not impossible.

Part Three

♥

You're Not Picky, You Just Know What You Want

Chapter Eight

You Know What's Best for You

I was dating a guy for a little while in college, and he seemed like the whole package," recalls Clare, 23. "He was very smart, attractive, had a lot of ambition, and was very well off. We got along fine, but there wasn't a lot of chemistry, and he ended up getting on my nerves. My friends and family all loved him and couldn't imagine why I was trying to get rid of him, so I stayed in the relationship awhile longer. I had convinced myself that I was being daft and didn't know a good thing when I had it. I spent a few more frustrating and uncomfortable months with him before we broke up. I don't know why I ever listened to them."

As much as we all want our boyfriends to be liked, if you ignore your own feelings about someone for the sake of your inner circle (or anyone else), you're settling. Your relationship should never be only about pleasing your friends and relatives. Of course you want them to approve of the guy, but ultimately, you have to please yourself. "I don't always make the best choices in men," Valerie confesses, "but I know better than anybody else who I like."

When I chose not to be with any of the men from *The Bachelorette*—Ben, Ryan, John Paul, or the twenty-two others—people made me feel terrible about it. They couldn't understand why I would give up on their favorite. I would hear comments like, "But Ben was so cute!," "Ryan was so sweet, why didn't you want to be with him?," "What's wrong with you for letting John Paul go?" On the surface, I can understand why they were confused. They were all great catches—incredibly nice, successful, smart, and good-looking. Like Clare, every time someone said anything to me, I began to second-guess myself. Was there something wrong with me because I didn't like this guy or that guy? They were all so great on paper . . . who wouldn't want a mate to have all of their fantastic qualities? I certainly do. But I had to remember that when people tell you, "He's great!," they're thinking about who *they* would like, not necessarily who *you* would like.

"Good on paper" doesn't always mean "good for me." Eighty-six percent of Americans say they wouldn't marry someone with the right qualities if they didn't love the person. What kept me from choosing these men was something no one else could see or feel: The chemistry was missing. The feeling you want to have when you're with a man just wasn't there. If there's no desire, nothing else matters. I wasn't going to force it with John Paul, Ben, or Ryan, and I wasn't about to let anyone else's opinion dictate how I felt. It makes no sense: They're not the one who has to deal with him on a daily basis. *You* are in the relationship. It's *your* life and *your* heart, and only you know what's best for you.

PARENTAL CONSENT

I don't buy the old adage "Mother knows best" when it comes to relationships. Sometimes she does, but sometimes she doesn't. Either way, you can't let her control your love life. "But my mother likes him" is as pitiful of an excuse for being with someone as "But all my friends are married."

Don't get me wrong, I want my parents to approve of the people I date. When I meet a new guy I find myself thinking, What's my mom going to say? Could my dad play golf with him? It's natural to want everyone in your life to get along, which is why many women tell me they let their parents influence their choices in men—but only to a certain extent. "I have given men a chance because those close to me have encouraged me to, or because he 'great on paper,'" says Dina. "But if I don't feel the chemistry I do not continue dating them." Chicago-based Amy shares a similar tact. "My friends and family are completely important to me, and their opinions matter," she acknowledges. "But at the end of the day, I'll always go with my gut."

The problem with relying on your parents' opinions is that their motivations aren't necessarily pure. Don't forget, mothers especially feel pressure from their friends to have a married daughter. Plus, your parents want you to be taken care of, and they probably come from a generation where chemistry was only important in science class. "My parents always berate me for being too picky and for having too-high standards," says journalist Andrea. "In fact, they repeatedly 'joke' to me, 'If he's Jewish and wears pants, there's nothing wrong with him.' This was only a tiny bit amusing when I was 20. Ten years and a thousand repetitions later, it's just flat-out annoying and insulting."

Some parents, unfortunately, seem to place more emphasis on their daughter's marital status than her actual happiness. I heard a story about a woman who told her father two days before her wedding, "I really don't want to marry this guy. Please don't make me do it." He did. And two years later, she got divorced. If only she listened to her instinct—and not her dad—she wouldn't have had to suffer so much heartache. Meanwhile, when designer Helen, 35, told her old-fashioned mother she was getting a divorce, her mom's reaction was, "Your father and I are praying for you to get back together with him." Helen says her parents think marriage is a holy decree that can't be broken; it didn't matter that their only daughter was suffering. "I lost a lost of weight in the last year of my marriage," says Helen. "I physically couldn't take it anymore." She told her mom the only thing she could: "Just pray for God's will and that's perfect for me."

DUTIFUL DAUGHTER

Wanting your parents and friends to like the guy you're dating is understandable. Dating a person *only* because you think they will like him is unwise. Remember Jenny from chapter 6? One major reason she stays in her unhappy marriage to Tom is because her family adores him. "I swear they like him more than they like me," she told me once. She's afraid if she leaves him it will upset her parents. Hello! *You* are their child. They can think he's great, they can be devastated to lose him. But at the end of the day, you're more important. As my mom says, "*You* are the one I love and your happiness is what matters most to me."

Relationship expert Dennie Hughes calls Jenny's type of behavior People Pleaser Syndrome. She explains, "Sometimes a woman only dates a guy because Mom loves him, and you feel so pleased that you pleased her." To ensure that you don't contract PPS, Hughes has two recommendations. First, "Shove thoughts of 'Mom would love him' or 'Mom would hate him' out of your head," she says. She's not dating him. Second, keep your guy away from influential people until you've formed a solid judgment of your own. "See if you like him without letting others opinions be a factor," Hughes says. If you don't wait, and everyone tells you he's amazing, there's a good chance you could be brainwashed to agree even when it's not how you really feel.

TRUTH OR CONSEQUENCES

I rely a lot on my friends for dating advice. They're good at telling me when I'm being neurotic and irrational; they keep me in check. Yet sometimes our friends can also be our worst enemies. When you ask them their opinion about a guy, a lot of times they will just tell you what they think you want to hear—which is usually, "He so great! We love him!" When I was on *The Bachelorette* and trying to choose between Jerry and John Paul, my friends Abby and Michelle came to visit me in New York and meet the guys. As it turned out, having them there only made the decision more difficult: They said they liked both men equally, but in different ways. Only after the show was all over and my decision was made did they tell me who they liked better. They said at the time they just didn't want to sway my opinion.

My mom and dad behave the same way. Like all good parents, they are always very supportive. And I love them for always acting like they're really fond of all my boyfriends. But, like clockwork, whenever I break up with someone, the first words out of my dad's mouth are either, "I never liked him anyway" or "I knew that guy wasn't right for you." Um, that would have been nice to hear at the time I was in the relationship. A few times, my mom has even said, "I can't believe you lasted as long as you did."

This just proves that your friends and family love you and often want to support you in spite of your best interest. Years ago, when recently divorced developer Fay tried to tell her friends that she didn't want to get married, they wouldn't listen. "They're natural cheerleaders," she says. When she would try to convince them the guy wasn't right for her, they would shoot back, "No, come on! You said that about the other guy. You're just afraid." Her conclusion: "Your girlfriends think that to be supportive is to be approving. No, to be supportive is to listen. And question, and probe. I wanted them to corner me in a room and say, 'What the f—?!' "

Before Valerie decided to leave her husband, she ran around to her inner circle and tried to gauge their opinions on her relationship. "In hindsight, I guess I was looking for people to support my decision, so when I decided to get divorced I knew I'd have a lot of support," she says. What she learned, however, was that no one backed her as much as she'd hoped. "I had a cousin who said, 'You're so lucky to have everything. I could never leave that.' But she didn't have to live it. I couldn't," she says. "In the end, their lack of support didn't matter because nobody else had to be married and nobody else had to get divorced."

EMBRACE THE P WORD

Friends—usually it's the married ones—often want to see you in a relationship so badly that they'll drop their standards for who you should date. That doesn't mean you should follow suit. "You *should* be picky," says relationship expert Dr. Jenn Berman. "It's your life." It's perfectly normal (and even good) not to fall for every guy you meet. Not long ago, I was at a party talking to a really attractive guy—who also happened to be the drunkest guest around. One of his close woman friends, an acquaintance of mine, asked me if I'd ever consider going out with him. I told her probably not, seeing how he was so wasted and was continuously yelling "Ay-Oh!" at the top of his lungs. Her response? "God, you *are* picky." *Really? That* makes me picky? I wouldn't have thought that not wanting to date an obnoxious alcoholic makes me picky. Excuse me for having standards.

When you suspect you're being sold out, it's okay to turn down dates. "A girlfriend's brother considered setting me up with a guy from his office," says Blair. "He had hardly anything good to say about him. He told me the guy wasn't good-looking, was kind of weird, and we probably didn't have a lot in common—but he was a genius and made a lot of money. My friend kept urging him to make the match, and I kept asking, 'Why do you want me to go out with this guy?' I was hurt thinking she wanted me to go out with a weird, unattractive guy.

It didn't matter to me how much money he had. I kept refusing to meet him, so they finally gave up."

Banker Shannon (who refuses to go on blind dates) has found that her friends constantly push certain people on her, even though she's not interested. One such guy: her boss. "People say things like, 'I don't understand why you guys just don't date.' They think we act like we're married," she explains. "It's my boss! I don't think it's appropriate. Nobody even cares how I feel, even though this is about me, not them."

By far, the worst example of "frenemy" (aka an evil friend) sabotage comes from Andrea: "One Saturday night, my gay male friend called me up and said, 'I'm going to a birthday party tonight and I think you should come with me. There are going to be a lot of interesting, single guys there for you to meet.' Fair enough. I figured he had my best interest in mind. Well, the party was my worst nightmare: a supercrowded New York City dance club. The guys there were mostly artsy and high. Why would I be interested in hooking up with—let alone meeting—any of these people? Suddenly, my friend took me into a corner and told me that he had made a revelation about my love life: I should have an affair with one of my male friends—who happens to be a happily married father of two. After I picked up my jaw from the floor, I told him that I would never, ever even consider such a thing. His reply? 'Plenty of couples meet this way. And if it's meant to be, it's meant to be.' I didn't know what was more offensive—that he actually encouraged me to date a married man, or that he thought I would be desperate enough to do it."

It really drives me crazy that these people think they are being helpful. They are just being nosy, rude, and unfair. They don't know what is best for you, only you do. I make an effort to tune out those annoying voices. I am confident that they have no idea what they are talking about.

However . . .

Do I think you should move through life *completely* ignoring other people's opinions? Not at all. It's worth paying attention to your nearest and dearest when they tell you a guy is *not* right for you. Sometimes, when you're so caught up in love, you'll tend to ignore red flags. (More on those in a few chapters.) If everyone around you is alerting you to the same thing—like your boyfriend is horrible to you or rude to others—chances are they're onto something.

BOTTOM LINE

If you have confidence in yourself and don't mind being single, you won't let anyone tell you who to date. "You should never have to be convinced," says psychotherapist Dr. Robi Ludwig. "You're not dealing with buying a car or a house. It's important to keep an open mind, but you can't help who you're going to be attracted to. It needs to be a combination of your head and your heart working together. It can't be one or the other, or there will be problems. When choosing a life partner, you have to be aware of realities: who you are and your goals and values." It doesn't matter how great he is on paper or how well he fits into your family. If it's not right *for you,* he's not right.

Chapter Nine

Don't Forget About the Frogs

*O*nce upon a time, *princess Blair was set up on a blind date with a potential prince named Todd.* "When I met him, I thought he was cute, funny, and seemed really cool," she says. "We had such a great time on our first date that after dinner, I called my friend who set us up and he and I both told her how well the night was going. We must have stayed out until 3 A.M. just chatting and laughing." *When Todd wanted to see Blair the next day, she didn't hesitate for a second. The day after that, he also wanted to do something.* "I thought that seemed a little intense, but I was smitten so I didn't question it," *she recalls.* "That first week, he confessed he'd never had anything like this happen before. He also said that one of his sisters even noticed something different when he was telling her about me. He seemed really genuine."

Blair and Todd continued to see each other over the next few weeks—but with less frequency. She chalked it up to busy schedules. "One Saturday, he went golfing and I said, 'Maybe we can

*do something tonight when you get back.' He agreed. But then he
didn't even call me until about 7 P.M. He said he was still in
New Jersey, wouldn't be back for a few more hours, and would be
too tired to go out. He didn't even seem to feel bad that he was
standing me up. I was upset, but I tried to tell myself it was no
big deal. He did call, after all."* Deep down, Blair knew things
weren't the same as they had been on those first few dates, but she
figured that's just what happens when you're in a relationship.
Soon enough, Todd stopped calling—no explanation, no nothing. *"When I realized what was happening, I spent the night in
tears. I was crushed,"* admits Blair, who quickly swore off dating
and even half-joked to her mother that she wanted to become a
lesbian. She continues, *"The next morning, I promised myself I
would never get caught up with a bastard like that again. I would
be more careful, and I wouldn't ignore signs of trouble. As much
as it sucked, I definitely learned a lot from this experience."*

She will, in turn, live happily ever after.

The end.

You're going to have to kiss (be hurt by, not called by,
played by—you name it) a lot of frogs before you find
your prince. "We don't know what's right until we've
dated a ton of people," says relationship expert Dennie
Hughes, "and most likely, nine out of ten will be wrong."
Blair learned this hard way—but then, haven't we all?

In the grand scheme of things, bad relationships aren't
such a terrible thing. In fact, they're enormously important. "They can be our best teachers and, in some ways,
our most valuable relationships," explains psychotherapist
Dr. Robi Ludwig. Not only do they help us grasp how

men operate, but they also act as a mirror onto ourselves. By understanding them, we can notice patterns in our own behavior that we need to change. Plus, they prove it's better to be single than sorry.

Now, I'm not saying I don't get heartbroken or sad when a relationship doesn't work out, but I know that breakups happen for a reason. The frogs I've come across have made me a stronger and more resilient (and more cautious) person. When a relationship goes awry, I don't panic as much as I did in the past; I know I can handle it. I'm not necessarily glad I dated certain men, but I have no regrets because without them I wouldn't know what I want from a boyfriend.

OLDER AND WISER

Instead of fretting that I didn't get married in my twenties, I look at being older and unmarried in a positive way: If you get married at 22, you've had so much less experience with men. At that age, I'd only had two serious boyfriends (one in high school and one in college). I was still sheltered and trying to establish myself as an adult; I was immature and utterly clueless about who I was. I can't even imagine what life would be like if I had married my college boyfriend like so many women do. When you're so young and inexperienced, how do you even know what an adult relationship entails? What are you willing to put up with? What kind of guy makes you the happiest? Says Sarah T., "When I think about the possibility that my 24-year-old self might have gotten married without all of the things I know about what I don't want in a man, I literally shudder."

I am a completely different person today than I was at 22 . . . and even at 25—the average age of marriage for an American woman. I can't say I've been intentionally waiting until I was out of my twenties to get married, but according to psychotherapist Dr. Jenn Berman, it's a smart move. "The thirties are when most women start to feel more confident and more comfortable in their lives," she says. "It's really an ideal time to meet a man." (An even better reason to hold off? Women between the ages of 25 and 29 have the highest divorce rates.) Says Rebecca (who wed at 32), "If I look back at who I dated at 27, I wasn't ready for marriage. The things I thought were important to me then and what's important to me now are really different. The older you are, the more you bring to the table. You have an identity. There's something nice about coming into a relationship with your own experience and your own life. I was away on a ten-day work trip and people asked, 'How are you going to deal being away from your husband?' I spent thirty-two years without Andy."

TAKE AIM

As much as we'd like to erase bad relationships from our memories, you have to learn from your mistakes. Berman offers the perfect analogy for this: "Relationships are like a bull's-eye," she says. "Each time you shoot the arrow, hopefully you get closer to the middle. How you get closer to the middle is by basing your next shot on your previous one." I fired a bad shot back in my twenties that has stuck with me to this day: I dated someone on and off for two years. I don't know if it was because I liked him so much or it was convenient, but we just kept going back to each other—even though the issues that kept breaking us up were never resolved. There was so much drama; it was exhausting. When it finally ended, I swore I would never do that again. And I haven't.

Since then I've also pledged not to stay in a relationship that I see going nowhere. I don't care if it's the summer, or it's the holidays, or whatever time of year it's nice to have a boyfriend (because there really isn't a good time to have or not have a boyfriend—you either want him around all the time or you don't). Also, while I always used to blame *myself* when certain things weren't working in a relationship, now I'm more confident in my actions. I'm at a point in my life where I can spot big issues right away and stop wasting months—even years—trying to fix them. All I have to do is remember how mad I got the last time around.

TRIALS AND ERRORS

Every woman has a different dating history, and we can learn from one another's experiences. Melissa used to always get upset when she wouldn't hear from someone after a date or two. "I don't take things so personally anymore," she says. "I've gotten tougher and more confident." Sarah L. learned to find a happy medium in her own behavior. "In my early relationships, I was too needy and desperate," she says. "Then in my later ones, I was too removed and detached. It took a little bit of both to find out what works for me."

Designer Dawn swears by the importance of listening to what men tell her on a first date. "When I was younger, I would hear things out of guys' mouths and make it into whatever I wanted it to be," she explains. "If a guy said he didn't want to have kids, I would have thought, I'll change him. Now, I hear what people say and take it at face value. When they say things like that, they mean it."

Jersey girl Carly dated her ex-boyfriend for three argument-free years. Ironically, she says she never wants a relationship like that again. "Both of us were compromising and doing things we didn't want to do just to avoid confrontation," she recalls. "When it ended, I decided I will fight with my next boyfriend—not because it's a bad relationship, but because arguing is so important; it shows passion. I won't even say I don't care about what we're watching on TV if it's not true."

Online daters have unique realizations of their own. "Every guy is at least two inches shorter than he says— usually more like five inches," Annalise tells me. "It always struck me as dumb to lie about something that you will instantly be found out about!" Similarly, Andrea has learned to "always assume they are displaying the Greatest Photo Ever." On a more serious note, Heather warns, "You need to be careful about men who are married and cheating or newly separated and not really ready to date. It's too painful and too much work." (Of course, that applies to men you meet offline, too.)

Sometimes, the most valuable lessons we learn are about ourselves. I know I'm not always blameless when my relationships turn sour. If you're an active participant in your own life, things don't just *happen* to you. Maybe I said or did something that turned him off. Anything is possible. Although I try not to overanalyze my breakups— sometimes the only answer really is that the guy is an ass—I do spend time reflecting on how it all played out. After a split, I give myself a cooling-off period, and then think about how *I* acted in the situation. (A good time to do this is when you're sitting in a pedicure chair staring off into space, or trying to push through the last ten minutes on the treadmill.) It could take months or years to truly see the error in your ways, but it does eventually pay off.

KNOWING YOUR MR. RIGHTS FROM MR. WRONGS

It hasn't been easy, but I'm learning to break my bad habits. Now that I'm older and wiser, I don't fall into the dating traps that snagged me in the past. For instance, I recently realized that I tend to fall for the same kind of men: really outgoing, type A personalities who exude an air of success and power. I always had the same complaints about them, which was that they had little time for me. It was as if all I had to do was insert a new name into my grumblings.

I now recognize that the man who is perfect for me is someone who can balance business with a personal life. I need a friend and a partner who wants to spend time with me rather than on his cell phone, and who isn't so preoccupied with his life that he can't relate to mine. Mind you, I'm not trying to find the total opposite—calling all shy, unmotivated losers—but just someone who is a better fit with my personality. It was so refreshing when I finally dated someone who didn't fit my typical profile. I remember at one point, he got wrapped up in moving and a new job, and I started feeling a little neglected. When I told him, he simply apologized and made a noticeable effort to make me a priority. I couldn't believe it was that easy. It made me realize there *are* men out there who will listen to me. (As it turns out, we broke up after a few months because we were better as friends, but I still see this as a step in the right direction.)

Fashion exec Valerie has repeatedly found herself in situations with men who didn't treat her well, but she admits she foolishly just ignored it. "I enjoyed my time with that person so much that I overlooked flaws," she says. "I got wrapped up in it. You forget. You think the wonderful feelings are going to outweigh the bad."

If she felt a guy was wavering in his feelings for her, she'd see it as a challenge. "It triggered a manic personality trait of mine that thought, 'I have to get him.'" After scaring a few men off, she says, "Now I'm committed to not being the one to push. If the person wants to be with me, they'll be with me. They'll call me. I'm not going to force myself on anyone."

Before Rebecca met her husband, she also had a history of dating guys who didn't appreciate her. "They took me for granted and weren't always there for me and supportive of me," she explains. "I was always to trying to accommodate them." Although she had suspected all of her exes had something in common, she didn't fully understand how poorly she had been treated over the years until she broke the pattern. "More than anything, you realize it once you find the right guy," she says. "You have this 'Aha!' moment."

To be fair, it would be wrong to prejudge every guy you meet just based on your past experiences. Saying something like "All guys are idiots" is like saying "All women are crazy." It's fine to be cautious, but also give people the benefit of the doubt. "I don't hold the difficulties or challenges of past relationships against the new men I'm involved with," says never-been-married Heather. "Your new man is not your old one." However, if you suspect he's the guy's clone, don't ignore that, warns Hughes. "If he sounds like the last guy you dated, get out."

NARROWING THE FIELD

Even though I haven't found The One yet, at least I know what I *don't* want in a person, which is good, too. It may limit my choice in men, but it's progress nonetheless. This way, when I do meet the right person I'll be able to say, "This is it. This is what I've been wanting." That's the beauty of not settling.

The things we put on our must-*not*-have list can range from the silly to the significant. I refuse to date someone who wears flip-flops but doesn't clip his toenails. Ew. I'm not expecting perfectly manicured toes on a man, but hygiene should count for something, shouldn't it? "I can't deal with high-maintenance guys, or guys who are at the gym more than anywhere else," says Boston-based Clare. "A nice body is great to look at, but incredibly boring to talk to." New Yorker Sarah D. has ruled out guys with low self-esteem. "The first serious relationship I had was with someone who I knew I'd always be more confident and successful than," she explains. "I don't want that—I want someone fearless. Now I know to choose someone who radiates confidence."

I often hear that one of the most annoying things about online dating is that a lot of time men don't pay attention to your wish list. For example, you say you're looking for an athletic nonsmoker age 26 to 34 who lives nearby, and an overweight 48-year-old who lives across the country writes to say he thinks you'd be perfect together. "Those check marks are there for a reason," says Andrea. "I want somebody I'm going to be compatible with. I don't think there's anything wrong with weeding out people." With so many men online, you *have* to be picky. "I've had about 5,000 e-mails in the past six months," Heather, who nixes anyone who posts a shirtless photo or has a screen name like "The Big One," tells me. "Some from out-of-state, different countries, two from women. One guy wanted me to try to get him a job in TV! I absolutely do not go out with all of them."

SPLIT DECISIONS

When I see friends go through major splits, it validates the fact that it's better to wait for the right person than make the person you're with right for now. I lived with Andrew for only six months, and I can attest to how difficult it is to disentangle your lives. Even the smallest things become an issue: Who gets to keep that picture? Who gets the chair we bought together? "It's so easy to get into a relationship, but it's much harder to get out of it," says Helen. "With marriage, all it takes is 'Will you marry me?' and then you go to the church and get married. But with a divorce, you're working with the laws, and financially, it can get very, very tricky. It's a delicate dance. Whatever you throw at them, they can easily throw back at you. There's also the emotional part of not having this person in your life anymore."

Living with someone is one of the biggest steps you can take in a relationship, and if there's one thing I got out of moving to San Francisco to be with Andrew, it's that I should have put more thought into my decision. After *The Bachelor* ended, it seemed like the right idea since we didn't want to have a long-distance relationship. I was so caught up in the romance of it all that I didn't think about what would happen if things between us didn't work out. I'd given up my apartment, my job, and everything I knew, so when it ended, I had to start my life again from scratch. (Still, that was more appealing than being miserable with each other.) Despite the difficulty, I won't say I regret the move. I learned so much from that experience, and now I'm prepared for the next time I move in with a man. I won't do it unless I know for sure we are getting married.

BOTTOM LINE

Every time I look back at my relationship history, I'm reminded of the famous quote "What does not destroy me, makes me stronger." I've been rejected. I've been hurt. I've survived so many jerks. But I'm still here, surrounded by fellow survivors whose tales keep me motivated. "My past mistakes completely and utterly changed me," relates divorcée Joanie. "My marriage was awful, but I never dwell on it. It's in the past and I have no bitterness. I moved on. But—and this is a big but—I now know that even if my current relationship fell apart to-morrow that I'll be okay on my own. I've got friends, talent, resources, and good skin! If I could survive that marriage I can pretty much do anything. I am less wor-ried now than I used to be, because I know I'm fine just by myself!"

Chapter Ten

Just Because He's . . .

*P*aula, 23, began dating Gerard, 29, after they met one night at a Baltimore restaurant. "He's a doctor," she coos. "He's very good-looking and very successful." Having only dated guys her own age who were making entry-level salaries, she was taken with his swanky lifestyle. "When we would go out, he would never make me chip in for anything," she says. "He eats at the best restaurants and wears nice clothes. He has two really nice cars—a Lexus convertible and a cool, pimped-out SUV with massaging chairs and a TV inside." He's also a recovering addict and a self-proclaimed narcissist. (He's a psychiatrist. He would know.) "There were times when he would treat me badly," she admits. "He would cancel plans. Or when we'd talk, he'd fixate on the fact that I have ADD and point out my insecurities, saying I was needy and that I had a daddy complex." They dated for a month, and then he dumped her. "Part of me wonders if I would have liked Gerard if he didn't have all the things he has," *she confesses. "I can be dazzled by that stuff. I don't go actively seeking it, but it's a nice perk."*

> *Just because he's rich . . .*
> *Just because he's cute . . .*
> *Just because he drives a nice car . . .*
> *Just because he's a doctor . . .*
> *Just because he's anything . . .*

. . . does not justify unacceptable behavior. If a man is being hurtful or just generally a dope, you should never make excuses based on superficial qualities.

LOOKS AREN'T EVERYTHING

The night I met Jerry on *The Bachelorette*, the first thing I thought to myself was, 'Wow. He is *hot!*' Really, the guy looks like he stepped out of the pages of *GQ*. When the moment came to have some one-on-one time with him, I was so excited. We headed upstairs to the sunroom and chatted for a while. I practically saw a glowing aura surrounding him.

That is, until our conversation ended and he suddenly scooped me up to carry me down the steps.

He thought he was being a gentleman (I was wearing four-inch heels), but I thought he was being a tool. It was such a cheesy, showy move. I was so turned off. As I was in his arms I thought, *Oh my God, I hate that he's doing this . . . but he's so cute.* I told myself to just block out what was happening. *I don't want him to be this kind of person. He's so cute. Just pretend it didn't happen.*

With my selective amnesia in full effect, I decided to keep Jerry around that night—and for the rest of the show. He's a nice guy, but frankly, my main rationale for wanting to be with him was physical attraction. It was so obvious that we didn't have a lot in common: I have a business degree; he has a spiritual adviser. He talks in abstract terms (and takes twenty minutes to answer a question); I am very black and white and to the point. I had no idea how to communicate with him. If it were any other guy, I never would have let our differences slide. But I just liked looking at him.

Obviously, physical attraction is important, but it shouldn't be the foundation of a relationship. Ask yourself, Am I letting this person do things I wouldn't let someone else get away with? There should never be a double standard. "If you let a man get away with bad behavior for any reason, you lower yourself in his eyes," says Denver relationship therapist Carolyn Bushong, L.P.C., author of *The 7 Dumbest Relationship Mistakes Smart People Make.* "If he's able to treat you disrespectfully in any way, that throws the relationship out of balance and, therefore, jeopardizes it long term."

FACING THE TRUTH

Call me superficial, but I'm not the first person to ever date someone for their looks. Confesses Katie, "I once

went out with a guy who fell asleep on our first date—
we were at the movies, at least—and I still wanted to go
out with him again. He was just so beautiful! Guys who
are cute enough can make you totally lose your head."
Annie dated an agoraphobic, possibly alcoholic tennis
pro because, she admits, "He was hot and he adored me.
It only lasted about two months." Sarah D. laments, "I
dated a guy who could barely form sentences and had no
sexual interest in me—or in women, I'm guessing—because he was absolutely beautiful and had a killer body.
I actually stuck it out for six months and *he* dumped *me*.
I was devastated."

You can't sustain a relationship on looks alone. "A
real relationship involves emotional connection," says
Bushong.

MAINTAINING STANDARDS

The one thing I can say about Jerry is that he always
treated me with respect. His behavior annoyed me, to be
sure, but I didn't feel like I was compromising my integ-
rity by being with him. I was just being silly. The real
danger in these situations arises when you're so infatu-
ated with a person's assets—physical and/or material—
that you (a) allow him to walk all over you or (b) stay in
an unfulfilling relationship because you don't want to
give up such a cute/rich/whatever (CRW) guy. (Yes, it
still qualifies as settling even if the man is as wealthy and
handsome as David Beckham.)

My friend Morgan fell into both of those categories during her five-year relationship with Eric, a lawyer from a well-to-do family. Eric's brothers were all doctors who lived in ritzy suburbs and had cute little wives who didn't have to work. That was the life Morgan wanted for herself.

Eric cheated on her pretty much the entire time they were together—the signs were there, but she just didn't want to see them. He partied a lot, put his friends and his own needs first, and treated her like crap. Once, when they were at a wedding, a well-endowed woman passed by their table and Eric turned to flat-chested Morgan and commented, "Those are boobies, Morgan. One day we'll get you some of those—and while we're at it, we'll have your nose fixed, too." Morgan is a very pretty woman who doesn't need plastic surgery. The sad thing is, she didn't even let his remark bother her. She put up with his behavior because, although things weren't perfect, in her mind eventually they would be. She was in love with the idea of what she thought her life would be like if she married him: a nice house, nice cars, and a summer home. She was so determined to live out this fantasy that the relationship only came crashing down after one of Eric's many conquests called Morgan to confess. Only then was she forced to face the facts and didn't have any other choice but to break it off. She was devastated to lose him, but I really think she was more devastated by the loss of what she thought her life with him could have been.

No one—I don't care what is at stake—should stay

with someone who is that big of a cad. Morgan deserved so much more, but at the time was lacking the self-esteem required to see the relationship clearly. It's the same reason why Sarah L. got in trouble in college. "I stayed in a relationship with a horrible guy just because I couldn't believe he was in a relationship with me," she recalls. "He was the cute, popular star of our college's sports team. He could have his pick of any girl in school. Of course, I later found out he was having many of them while he was dating me. I stayed in the relationship because I stupidly thought it was better to have a boyfriend, even a bad one, than it was to be alone. When I finally broke up with him, I realized how much better and stronger I was on my own."

It's hard not to be blinded by stars. Makeup artist Liza, 35, was once in a relationship with a famous Hollywood director and admits, "Fame, power, and money can be aphrodisiacs." When they began their relationship, Mr. Director was already seeing another woman, "but he told me he was going to break up with her when he was done filming," Liza recalls. She convinced herself things would work out between the two of them. As she puts it, "We really were joined at the brain." Still, he would go away to film on location and never call her. "His personality was so powerful, but he was an asshole," she says. "I thought, You're not going to meet a guy like him every day, so I put up with it. I was in a trance, a fantasy." Here's how bad it got: She found out their relationship was over when she read in a newspaper that he had gotten married. Screams Liza, "He dumped me without telling me!"

Liza didn't even seem to care that she was compromising her morals by getting involved with Mr. D. while he was dating another woman. New Yorker Alexis, 32, once dated a married man and acknowledges, "In a million years I wouldn't have done that if he wasn't cute and unbelievably wealthy. He told me he was unhappy with his wife and he was leaving her, but I think I let the money—and especially the attention he gave me—cloud my mind." Needless to say, that man's marriage is still intact and Alexis is still single.

STRIP AWAY THE FACADE

Just because someone has money or looks doesn't make them a good person. If he isn't there for you emotionally and he doesn't respect you, what good do all the riches in the world do? Take the man off the pedestal and see him for who he really is. "It is important to search for a man's flaws immediately so you can protect yourself against them," advises Bushong. "And knowing them will help you not be intimidated so you can be an equal partner in the relationship."

Something that really bothers me is how we'll recognize the error of our ways for a moment, and then choose to let things slide. (This was exactly what happened with Jerry.) We're too forgiving and easily forgetful. Listen to your gut. Deep down, you know what you're doing.

Morgan knew she was being disrespected, but she chose to ignore it as Eric would sweet-talk her and make her feel crazy for feeling the way she did. The sad thing is, her other friends and I all told her he was a jerk many times; his excuses always trumped our caring disapproval. She believed what she wanted to because that was easier to deal with than the thought of breaking up.

Keep your eyes open when you're in a relationship. If everyone around you is telling you the *exact* same thing—"Yes, he's hot. But he's a real bastard"—don't say, "What? I don't know what you're talking about," and turn the other cheek. Pay attention. Chances are they're not blinded by his charm the way you are.

BECOMING ATTRACTIONS

It's a wonder how often we use something like a vacation home or even a foreign passport to talk ourselves into liking a guy more than we really do. Or worse, we use them as reasons to overlook behaviors we would normally never accept. Not too long ago, I dated a man whose parents had places in Cape Cod and Santa Barbara. I knew from the beginning I didn't like him, but I thought, Well, my beach wedding would be really pretty. Maybe I should give this guy a little longer to grow on me—and I did. The only thing I got out of the extra time was a feeling of boredom. I had to be honest with myself: The spark just wasn't there. I was staying with this guy not because of who he was but because of what he possessed. It was wrong (I am not a gold digger) and a waste of time to continue dating him. Good-bye seaside nuptials.

Lynn, a 33-year-old historian, once dated a rich eccentric whose family owned a waterfront home in Newport, Rhode Island. "He was in my circle of friends, but he was so odd that I wouldn't even admit to people that we were a couple," she says. "I wasn't into being his girlfriend, but I imagined myself living this fabulous life and that made dating him fun." Meanwhile, Carly admits she tried dating someone just because his family vacationed in Maine—her favorite place. "I usually wouldn't go out more than once with someone I had nothing in common with," she says, "but this time I focused too much on unimportant things we had in common. I tried to make everything else fall into place." That never works.

Blair once was captivated by a Frenchman at a friend's birthday party. "He was good-looking, worldly, fun, and, of course, had a cool accent," she explains. "He pursued me hard, which was very flattering—and also funny: When we would talk on the phone, I didn't always understand what he was saying." Off the bat, she knew to be careful because she'd heard he'd just come out of a long-term relationship. "I was afraid I was the rebound girl," she says. "I knew not to get too attached, but I had to live out this fantasy."

Frenchie, as she and her best friend like to call him, wasn't perfect. He smoked a lot. A LOT. For Blair, who has never even held a cigarette to her lips, this was a big deal. "I hate smoking," she says. "Until then, I said I would never date a smoker." He also rode a motorcycle around the city. "Yet another thing I never planned on doing," she notes. Still, he was nothing like the American men she's dated. "He was romantic. He complimented me on my clothes. And he was *French*! I found the whole thing very entertaining." One night, the pair went out for dinner to a little bistro where Frenchie knew all the staff. Throughout the meal, he kept making her get up with him to go outside to the garden (which wasn't open yet—it was still pretty chilly) so he could smoke. "We must have gotten up four times," she recalls. "It was getting really annoying, but I kept telling myself, He's French! Who cares?!" But she did. She knew this relationship wasn't going to last, so she figured she'd just enjoy it while she could . . . which was one more date. "That night, he paid more attention to the female bartenders than he did to me. At that point, his French charm lost its appeal. He didn't call me ever again, but I was okay with it. In fact, my lungs and I were actually pretty relieved."

BOTTOM LINE

I'm not trying to take the fun out of dating. By all means, if you meet a CRW and you want to go on a couple dates with him for fun—and, perhaps, to have people look at you with envy—fine. We all deserve a good time. Just keep your emotions under control and don't use a list of superficial reasons as an excuse to fall for him. Don't throw all of your standards out the window or let superficial things—a foreign accent, a beach house, smooth talk—distract you from what you really want. Keep a level head and don't overlook the importance of good character.

Chapter Eleven

Don't Talk Yourself into Liking a Guy

I've never had such a bad reaction to a guy than I did with
*Alan," graduate student Rachel A., 26, tells me. "We met
at a bar. I wasn't attracted to him, but when he called me a few
days later, I'd forgotten about that. All I thought was, A date!
I'll go."* On their first night out, he took her to a nice restaurant
and on a tour of the city. She learned he was sweet, ambitious,
and well educated. *"If he saw a flower dying in the street he
would pick it up so it didn't get run over,"* says Rachel. *"He
was such a great guy. I felt like I should like him—I thought I'd
grow to like him."* They began a relationship, but her feelings
didn't change. *"Here was a guy who was so into me and so nice
to me. I thought I was being immature by not liking him back.
My mom even loved him, and her approval means a lot to me.
I had to keep trying to like him."* As the months passed, however, the only feeling she cultivated was disgust. *"I was so
mean,"* she confesses. *"I would always break plans. He would
write me massive e-mails and I would write back a line. He*

would want to make out and I would pull away. I didn't like the way he smelled. He grossed me out." Literally. One after-noon, when Rachel was waiting for Alan to pick her up—he had gotten tickets to a concert in a nearby city—she was so dis-tressed that she threw up. "I became physically sick because I couldn't bear the thought of being in a car with him for an hour and spending the night together," she explains. Finally, she broke up with him. "He was so upset," she says. "But I was so relieved."

Every guy I've ever dated I've liked immediately. When I've tried to talk myself into liking someone, it's never worked out. (I can't say I've actually thrown up because of it, but I've definitely felt queasy.) Like Ra-chel, I've tried to be open-minded and keep things go-ing. I've told myself, He's such a great catch, maybe it's me, maybe if I give it more time he'll do something to knock my socks off . . . I've never changed my mind. All that kind of thinking ever does is prolong the misery while you dream of igniting a spark that was never there. It's a waste of time and at this point in my life, I would never continue something I knew for sure wasn't right from the start. I love myself too much to put my-self through that torture.

When I meet a guy, what's more important than how he looks, what he does, or what kind of shoes he wears is whether or not we have chemistry. I'm not talking I-want-to-rip-your-clothes-off-right-now chemistry. What I mean is, does he energize me? Does it feel comfortable being together? Do I want to spend time with this person? These feelings are relationship requirements and they cannot be manufactured. Sure, a person can grow on you, but if you're repulsed, that's not going to change. It's not like it's just going to click one day. That only happens in the movies.

If you have to convince yourself that you like a man, you're settling. It doesn't matter how great he is, or how hard you're trying. The end result, warns relationship expert Dennie Hughes, is that "you will never be happy." Plus, it's just not fair to the guy. "You do him a huge disservice," she says. "Would you want to date someone who didn't really like you?"

FIRST IMPRESSIONS

The way to prevent talking yourself into liking a guy is to pay attention to how you feel on your first date—or even before. Dawn tells me that when she finally has a phone conversation with a guy she meets online, it can be quite enlightening. "The transition from phone to e-mail reveals a lot," she explains. "You discern insecurities, lack of maturity, bitterness from previous failed relationships and an obsession with the candy store aspect of online dating." Your initial reaction means something; trust it. Research has shown it takes most people between ninety seconds and four minutes to decide if they like a person. "You need to know where you stand on first impressions," explains psychotherapist Robi Ludwig. "Some people know how they feel right from the get-go. Others don't know right away." (The more men you meet, the more you can practice honing this skill.) For Lea, the answer comes before the first drink has been ordered. "I think for blind dates, you can tell within the first few minutes whether they are right for you or not. There has to be a physical connection for there to be fire. In a few cases, someone's sense of humor or personality has changed my opinion of them, but I have developed nothing more intense than a harmless crush." Agrees Washington, D.C.–based Catherine E., 27, "If there is no chemistry in that first date, I know there's never going to be any. It isn't something you should ignore—if it's not there, it's not going to appear overnight."

The worst thing is when you have chemistry before the date—in online chats or phone calls—and then discover there's no real spark when you're face-to-face. Says former online dater Annalise, "When you meet people, you often realize they were probably sitting in front of their computers for hours crafting witty responses—or having their friends do it." The whole experience can be even more disappointing than not clicking with a blind date. "There is no turning back at that point," says online dater Lisa. "Once you meet someone in person, you cannot return to the image that you had of him before."

Of course, you're not *always* going to be 100 percent certain about every man you meet. You know you're not repelled (which is good), you know there's a bit of chemistry (also good), but you're also not dying of excitement. My rule: If I'm unsure but still intrigued, I keep seeing him. Curiosity is a form of attraction. It took four dates for Patty to decide she liked her now-husband. "He wasn't my type at all," she admits, "but there was just *something* about him that captivated me. I knew I wasn't forcing it, though, because I never felt like, ick, what am I doing?" As ivillage.com dating expert Sherry Amatenstein notes, "Great relationships can grow gradually after time. But you can't force yourself if you're gagging at the thought of being with someone."

As Dawn sees it, "There has to be some kind of spark to make you want to go out with him again. Just because he's a living, breathing thing isn't enough." Usually, she says, she can gauge a guy's potential on the first date, although she's also aware that sometimes her mood can affect her perception. "I felt one first date was going nowhere, and then I realized I was playing some part in that. I was thinking of other things. As soon as I let my guard down, that changed instantly. He was a great guy." Another man, however, has her stumped. "I'm not so attracted to him but I enjoy sitting there talking to him," she says. "He's smart, has a ton going for him. He's worth giving another chance, but I'm not going to push myself into being with him. If I know by the end of that date or the next that it's not there, so be it."

In one survey, 56 percent of women said they would go on a second date with a man hoping for chemistry to develop. Again, what's essential here is that you're not going out with someone you *don't* like; you're going out with someone you *might* like. There's a big difference. "I believe in listening to your instinct," says psychotherapist Dr. Jenn Berman. "If you go on a date with someone and you really have an instinct that this is not the person for you, there's no reason for you to waste your or his time. If you're on the fence, then go, definitely. It doesn't have to be love at first sight, but if you dread the idea of seeing him again, you should not be going out with him." Relationship expert Dennie Hughes offers another perspective: "Even if on the first date there are no sparks, but the guy is nice and not a jerk, give it another shot." If the guy is awkward and a little nervous, that's not necessarily a bad thing, she says. "He's probably more sincere—the ones that are good at the first date may be guys that specialize in first dates!" notes Hughes. "By the second date, because you gave him another chance, he will probably be less nervous."

I can't fake interest in a person (something *Bachelorette* viewers witnessed—I had no I idea how much my face gave away what I was feeling inside), which is why I will only go out on second (third, fourth . . .) dates if I feel the chemistry is already there. Aside from being uncomfortable, going out with people you don't like is work. Trying to seem interested for two or more hours is exhausting. When I've tried to "give him a chance," as my friends often urge me to do, I never act like myself—I'm pleasant, but totally boring and have a difficult time making conversation. Then, the guilt rolls in as I realize I am looking at this person and only thinking about how awful he is and how soon I can go home. Life is so much less stressful if you go out with men because you want to, not because you think you have to.

NO BUTS

There are so many different reasons—that is, lame excuses—why women will try to talk themselves into liking a man. I've foolishly agreed to dates in an attempt to refute the charges that I'm picky. (I'm sure the guys would have loved to hear this: "I like you because I'm not selective.") At a certain point, I just can't take it anymore and I start resenting the person, even though he's done nothing wrong.

Be honest with yourself. Don't express emotions that don't exist in your heart. You have talked yourself into liking a guy if you find yourself saying or thinking, "I'm not really into him, but [insert one of the phrases below]."

"HE'S A GOOD GUY"

Let's be honest: No one ever tries to talk herself into liking an asshole. Usually in these situations, you're dealing with a person who is a gentleman, interesting, has a good job, a sense of humor, and is decent-looking. You really can't find anything wrong with him, so you overlook the little fact—*the most important fact*—that you're not attracted to him.

"I tried to talk myself into liking a guy who was all the things I should have wanted: funny, nice, Jewish, and successful—and he liked me," recalls Rebecca. She went out with him three times but could never reciprocate his feelings for her. "I ended up feeling really bad because I didn't have a quantifiable reason why I didn't like him," she says. "I felt very guilty about it. You think it's very superficial."

Ashley uses some of the exact same words to describe her own experiences. "I used to date men who I wasn't necessarily attracted to, but they met all of my checklist items," she admits. "I felt guilty and superficial for not giving them a chance, but it never worked." She'd often find herself getting caught in a vicious dating cycle. "I'd be really nice because I'd feel bad that I didn't like him, so then the guy would inevitably call to ask me out again."

As I've said before, you're not going to like every guy you meet, "good guys" included. There's nothing wrong with that. Instead of feeling guilty for *not* liking him, maybe you should feel guilty about stringing him along. "You have to be willing to let go of guys who aren't right for you," says Berman. "That's one of the hardest things of dating. Nobody wants to hurt someone else's feelings." Most people equate breakups with fighting, she adds, "but sometimes you can be in a relationship with a really terrific guy who's wonderful but he's just not the right match for you. It's important to honor yourself and him and the relationship by getting out if it's not the right thing for you."

"I'VE INVESTED SO MUCH TIME IN THIS"

This is a common excuse among online daters. They spend hours on their computers every night, and weeks trading e-mails with guys they'd like to date—and they want a payoff. But it doesn't always happen. Andrea once spent *six months* communicating with a guy before they got together in person. They hit it off so well in e-mails and on the phone that she had convinced herself he was the perfect guy for her. When they finally met, she quickly realized that wasn't the case at all—but she went out with him again (and convinced herself she'd be okay wearing flats for the rest of her life) because their online relationship had gone on for so long. "Never e-mail with a guy for a prolonged period of time," she now warns. "The buildup and expectations get too high. It's like when you hear great buzz about a movie for months and then, after finally seeing it, you realize it was just a bunch of publicity hype and you want a refund." The best way to prevent this from happening is not to drag out an e-relationship; once you connect online, plan to meet as soon as possible.

"I LIKE THE ATTENTION" OR
"I LIKE HAVING A BOYFRIEND"

Many women are so insecure that no matter who likes them, they'll reciprocate. When I was in college, I was friendly with a girl who dated every different type of guy on campus—jocks, stoners, business majors, you name it. I could never figure it out. She couldn't possibly like *all* of these men. Wasn't she in the least bit particular? Finally, I realized it wasn't about the guy at all: She just liked the attention and liked having a boyfriend. It's easy to talk yourself into liking someone if you're unhappy being single. (If that's the case, reread chapter 1.) Explains Alexis, "I excuse a lot at the beginning of a relationship because I want it to work out. It's the desperation of wanting to be in something." You can overlook things like clothes or his haircut, but never excuse a lack of chemistry.

"WE CAN DOUBLE DATE"

My friend Mandy is constantly trying to set me up with one of her boyfriend Barry's friends. She says, "Wouldn't it be so great? We could all be friends forever!" Yes, it would be great—*if* I was attracted to the guy. For some women, it's tempting to date (and talk themselves into liking) someone within their social circle. It was certainly something Shannon considered when she went out with a former college classmate. "It would have been perfect because his friends were my friends," she says. "We could have gone out as couples all the time. On top of that, we even liked a lot of the same things, like baseball. But when you got down to it, when it was the two of us, we didn't have that much to talk about."

"I DON'T WANT TO DISAPPOINT MY MATCHMAKER"

One reason why blind dates are so tricky is because they involve three people: you, your date, and the person who set you up. Sometimes we feel so much pressure for a setup to be a success that we'll force ourselves into dating guys we know we don't like. "My dad's boss set me up and I didn't like the guy, but I thought I had to keep going out with him because I didn't want it to reflect badly on my dad," says Melanie. When you continue to date someone for the sake of your matchmaker, all you're doing is getting that person's hopes up. (The guy's, too.) Plus, you also run the risk of looking like a bitch when you finally end it.

Learn a lesson from Corinne. She and Phil were set up by their grandmothers, who were friends. "All I was told was that he was 'a very nice young man,'" she says. She knew going into the date that if it didn't work out, she'd have a lot of explaining to do. "The first time I saw him was when he was walking down the street to pick me up in front of my apartment building. He was fine looking—I didn't think, Yes!, but I guess it could have been worse."

There was, however, one big problem. "He walked like a duck," she says. "I really have a problem with men who walk with their feet pointed outward. I tried to be nonjudgmental and overlook it." At dinner, she noticed a chain around his neck. "Yet another turnoff," she admits. Over the course of conversation, she learned they had a few things in common, "but I definitely wasn't thinking anything romantic. At all."

Nevertheless, when Phil called her for another date, she said yes. "I didn't want to let down my granny, and I was trying to be adult and give him a chance. I thought maybe I'd see something different in him this time." They had dinner and then went to a bar where Corinne had gone with an ex-boyfriend. "Despite the fact that my ex ended up having major issues, I couldn't help but sit there dreaming I was there with him and not Phil."

He asked her on a third date. "At this point, the mere thought of him creeped me out, but I felt bad saying no. After all, he was a nice guy. I wanted everyone in my family to know I gave him a chance." At the movies, she sat with her hands folded in her lap the entire time be-cause she was scared he might try to grab one. Afterward, they had dinner at a restaurant that served all-you-can-drink wine. "Let's just say I took advantage of that. It was the only way I could deal," she confesses. "I stumbled out of the restaurant thinking how badly I wanted to go home. As we stood waiting for the light to change, he took my hand. Deep down, I shuddered. I thought, *This can't be happening. Please make this stop!* When we got to the street that led to his apartment, he asked me if I wanted to come over. I didn't want to hurt his feelings, so I said yes. Things got worse at his apartment when he put the moves on me. Honestly, I hooked up with him out of pity. After a little while, I told him I had to leave. I went into the bathroom and imagined throwing up. I felt so awful about myself for letting it get to this point. I didn't even want him to come downstairs to put me in a cab, but he was being a gentleman, so he did. A few days later, when he called to chat, I had to tell him I didn't want to see him again. I lied and said I wasn't over my ex-boyfriend ('I knew there was something,' he replied) and I needed to sort things out before getting involved with someone else. After that incident, I never tried to force myself to like a person. I'm nauseous just thinking about it."

How did Corinne's grandmother take the news that the relationship didn't work out? "She was surprisingly cool about it," she says. "She told me, 'Well, I tried.' All that agony for nothing!"

"I DON'T WANT TO HURT HIS FEELINGS"

This excuse is at the root of many of those mentioned above. Simply put, don't be so nice. You're actually being mean if you're leading someone to believe you want to be dating him. "So many women suppress the 'something just doesn't feel right about him' instinct because they are raised to be polite, and kind, and to not hurt someone's feelings," explains Hughes. "If someone makes you feel totally icky, end the date and don't see him again."

DON'T AGONIZE

If you can't figure out if a guy is right for you after a few dates or a few weeks, he's not. Stop wasting your time. The longer you let a relationship drag on, the harder it is to end. (The last thing you want to do is to wake up in a few *years* and realize the spell you put on yourself has worn off.) Never be afraid of being alone.

Special projects manager Elizabeth, 30, follows a three-date rule: "If after three dates I still feel uninspired and there's no sign of weakness in my knees, time to delete his info from my BlackBerry," she says. "It's about chemistry—not just physical attraction, but that intangible quality that makes you understand a person and feel completely comfortable at all times." Adds Carly, "A lot of time when you go out with people you're giving a second or third chance to, it's not a natural chemistry. It's a friendship that has some hooking up in it."

"You can only fool yourself for so long," says chef Sheila. "I was in a relationship with a great guy, Mark. He adored me, but he was too much for me at that time. I tried to tell him we needed to take it easy." Her actions, however, spoke louder than her words. "I went out with my friends and ran into a German guy that I had flirted with a bit, and Mark walked into the bar as the German and I were kissing," she recalls. "Either you take the plunge and break things off, or else you will do something to sabotage it yourself."

BOTTOM LINE

If you're a strong person, you will be okay letting go. As Jessica Simpson said after her breakup with Nick Lachey, "[You] just have to realize that if you're not happy, you can't make anybody else happy. When you walk away from something and there's no gravitational pull, then you know you're doing the right thing."

These may sound ridiculous to friends and family, but when you know what you want, why settle for anything less? (And yes, these are all real.)

- "He took me to an outdoor event in the rain."
- "He left voice mails in different accents."
- "He wore a retainer."
- "He wore mandals, shorts, and a braided belt."
- "His hair was crunchy."
- "His hair smelled like bad cheese."
- "He told me I reminded him of his mom."
- "He signed every e-mail with 'Peace in the Middle East.'"
- "He talked to his parents on the phone at least two hours a day, and they lived less than ten miles away."
- "He wore a blousy leather jacket with an elastic waistband."
- "He spoke these words: 'My biggest passion in life is being a thespian.'"
- "He drove a hybrid car and gave the corresponding lecture."
- "His beanbag chair drove me crazy."
- "He had a really ugly comforter. It had brown

flowers and it was cheap and shiny. It looked like it was from Motel 6."

✦ "His breath smelled like he'd just scarfed down a salami sandwich."

✦ "He was just too nice and polite and never went in for a kiss—even after five dates."

✦ "His apartment was so messy that I was freaked out something would crawl out of the piles of clothes and newspapers."

✦ "He was so small that if I imagined us piling into the backseat of a car, he'd end up on *my* lap."

✦ "He had no neck."

✦ "He showed up to my house one night wearing enormous, light blue sneakers. They freaked me out."

✦ "He had way too much cover-up on a pimple."

✦ "He didn't think my jokes were funny."

✦ "He had a bad last name."

✦ "He wore white leather sneakers."

✦ "He wore high-tops."

✦ "His jeans looked like they were from the late nineties."

✦ "He wore bracelets."

✦ "We went to see *Star Trek: The Next Generation,* and he pumped his fists in the air in excitement when the *Starship Enterprise* went across the screen."

✦ "He told me he BROKE his penis and it was out of commission for a few days."

Part Four

♥

In Search of That Elusive Feeling

. . . .

Chapter Twelve

"You Know When You Know," What the Hell Does That Mean?

*M*y husband, Jake, will gleefully tell you that according to *my diary—which he snooped and read—I had decided by our second date that he was the guy I was going to marry,"* says writer Francine, 40. *"But that only answers the question of when I knew. The why and how isn't so easy. We took a vacation nine months into our relationship, and it was amazing to me how well we traveled together. That trip definitely helped to form the opinion that we functioned well as a unit, but it was also all the little things along the way and since that trip that convinced me he was the right man to be with for the rest of my life. I realized that our temperaments complemented each other, our quirks were not going to drive the other one crazy, and our interests and opinions were rather compatible. Everything clicked. I hate to present you with a trite idea but it's really true: You just know."*

Ah, those three little words. They're all I ever hear when someone is trying to tell me what it feels like to realize you've found The One. Obviously, I'm not expecting anyone to tell me that a plane flew by pulling a banner that said, "This is the guy!," but as someone still in search of the man I'm going to marry, this "you know" thing really puzzles me. (I have a hard enough time liking a pair of shoes I just brought home from the store—and I thought I was in love with them, too.) What do you know? How does it feel? Does everyone "know"? I say I'm looking for this myself, but I worry I won't be able to identify it. Sometimes, I'm scared that maybe it doesn't even exist.

SPOTTING FAKES

At this point, I'm not sure I fully believe in the whole "you know when you know" concept, but I suspect that's because I haven't experienced it yet. Or rather, I thought I'd experienced it at certain moments in my life, but it turned out I was wrong. That same guy I imagined marrying years ago I now consider to be one of the most annoying people on the planet. The thing that really bugs me, though, is how did I not see that before? How was I so fooled?

Just as pregnant women can have a false contraction, women in search of The One can have a false "I know." Over the last few years, I've had so many friends tell me "This is it!" only to end up single again six months later. My friend Lindsay, 30, is engaged now, but twice in the past she believed she was dating her future husband. The

first time was in college. "If I don't marry Billy, who-
ever it is will have big shoes to fill," she explained.
(They broke up before senior year.) A few years later,
she was "so in love" with a man who lived out of town.
"It's so true when they say you just know," she told me
with a perma-grin. "It's him. I just know it." He broke
up with her a few months later.

Celebrities, it seems, are the worst at knowing when
love is real. I can't even count how many times I've
heard Paris Hilton gush about how she was "so in love"
with a number of different guys. Then there's Angelina
Jolie, who said during her marriage to Billy Bob Thorn-
ton, "[I] knew it was true love because I kept walking
into walls. That's the kind of daze I was in. My love for
him is deep. It's like the love you feel for your family,
but it's more. You know you really will spend the rest of
your life with this person, which is an amazing, calming
feeling." They divorced after three years. Oops, I guess
she really didn't know.

According to Dennie Hughes, "People confuse major
attraction—a really powerful feeling—with love." Usually this occurs within the first few months of a relationship, when both people are on their best behavior and
everything seems so great, so exciting, and so perfect.
This is when we get all sappy and annoying and can't
think of anything but our boyfriends. Interestingly, sci-
entific research has shown that the chemicals released in
the brain during this phase of love are the same ones
triggered by cocaine and nicotine. "This attraction can

be an infatuation," says dating expert Sherry Amatenstein. "You have to see if it's reality versus a fantasy, and
that takes time." And like a high, the attraction stage—as
we've all learned—doesn't stick around forever. A long-
lasting partnership requires attachment, which takes time
to build. (In this phase, hormones that promote bonding
are released in the brain.) A relationship isn't legit, says
Amatenstein, "until you really know each other, get
through things together, and know how you fit into each
other's lives. It's not going to last if attraction is all you
have."

WHO KNOWS

Although I haven't had my relationship epiphany yet, I
have figured out the combination of things that I imagine will get me there: I'll feel at ease with my boyfriend.
He'll make me happy. He'll laugh with me. He'll be my
best friend. He'll see all the good in me, and all the bad,
and he'll love me anyway. I won't care that other men
exist because I won't be able to imagine being with anyone else. Even when things are rough, I'll want this
person by my side. I don't expect all of this to happen
within the first month of a relationship, or even the first
three months (and certainly not on the first date, so I've
stopped putting that pressure on myself). For most people, "knowing" is a slow process of realization over an
extended period of time. I'm willing to wait it out.

However, just so I don't miss it, I decided to ask

women who have experienced this romantic realization to share their insight. I'll start with Long Island native Sarah M., 26, who tells me she knew her husband, Chris, was The One long before they even began dating. "Chris was a senior when I was in eighth grade," she explains. "My friend Meg and I had major crushes on him and his classmates. When he would wait on me at his father's fish market, I would freak out. In some way I knew, regardless of if he had a girlfriend, that if I ever got involved with him—and if somehow he ended up as interested in me as I was in him—then that would be it." When they finally began dating the summer before her senior year in college, she says, "I knew even more. There were signs all over the place, similarities that we had that I had never had with anyone, let alone my old boyfriends: We were from the same hometown, had the same values—even the same flip-flops. In a world full of Reef wearers, we both wore Redleys. We both had grown up with cats, not dogs. We were both really active, and we ran the exact same grass course at our high school. It seems weird, but all these little signs pointed to why I knew he was The One." Although they made no commitment to each other when Sarah headed back to college, they ended up talking on the phone every day—"not because we felt some sort of obligation," she explains, "but because we wanted to connect with each other, like we had done during the last two weeks of the summer." When Sarah would see her old boyfriend walking around campus with his latest girlfriend, she'd think about how her connection to Chris was so much stronger than anything she'd had with the ex. "At one point, my old roommate and good friend, Brett, said to me, 'Admit it, Sarah, Chris is your boyfriend!' And as much as I wanted to roll my eyes at her statement, I could not deny my intense physical, mental, and spiritual connection to Chris. He *was* my boyfriend. I knew it would be that way forever, and it made me happy." They had a hometown wedding a few years later. "Chris wore flip-flops," she says. "It was incredible."

Okay, so most people probably don't have things figured out when they're still teenagers. For Amy, remembering the frogs she met during adulthood helped her recognize when she'd found the perfect guy for herself. "It has to do with experience—trial and error, so to speak," she says. "I had three long-term, serious relationships prior to meeting my husband. Every one of them was a learning experience and made me realize what I didn't want. I always thought that phrase 'when you know you know' was B.S., but after three weeks with him, I knew. We were engaged two months later." Francine, now married for five years, explains, "You say to yourself that this person is everything I want and fulfills all my needs, or he fulfills enough of them to make me happy." Sheila describes "knowing" as "something inside of you feels 'at home.'" Banker Katherine, 27, who has been in a relationship for two years tells me, "You know when one day it occurs to you that you can't imagine your life without him." Carly's simple explanation for how she knows her boyfriend of a year is The One: "He's the first person I've been willing to discuss bathroom things with."

Although Denver-based Jamie, 33, concedes, "I don't think you can really understand 'knowing' until you find the right person," she does have a valuable lesson to share. "The last serious boyfriend I had before meeting my husband was an amazing guy by any standards," she says. "But I spent so much time hoping and wanting him to be the guy when really my gut knew that he wasn't. If you have to think about it over and over again, and then question it over and over again, he isn't the right match for you. Real love is more obvious."

Newlywed Liz agrees. "When it's right, it is easy," she says. "When I met my future husband, there was no bad drama and no pressure. There wasn't a particular 'aha' moment, but this building of little things. Usually, you're building a pile of good things and bad things and at some point the bad things pile up so high they tip over into a breakup. With us, the good things piled up so high they spilled into a committed relationship and marriage."

Then again, as Rebecca learned, it's not always good things that bring you to the point of awareness. Just six months into her relationship with Andy, he was diagnosed with a potentially fatal illness. "A lot of people said to me, 'If you're not into this, you should walk away,'" she recalls. "I realized I would rather have what limited time I had with him than a whole life without him. Yes, I was put into a bizarre situation where I had to think that way, but I just knew this was the person I was supposed to be with." Not only is he completely healthy now, but they've already celebrated their first anniversary.

NO KNOWS

As hopeful as these stories make me, there are still plenty of women out there who don't believe in the "you know when you know" concept. "Every time I've fallen for someone I've had that moment where I've thought, This is it," admits Valerie, whose romantic history includes a broken engagement to one man, a failed marriage to another, and a handful of postdivorce boyfriends. "And obviously, it still isn't it. Whatever that moment is, I still haven't felt it." So does that mean she's doomed to an unhappy marriage or a life alone? Not at all. In fact, it's quite possible to be happy and secure in a relationship without having an "aha!" moment.

"I'm in the thirteenth month of a great relationship," says beauty industry executive Kit, 28. "I've never had a big, revelatory moment—and I feel slightly inadequate about it. But he is the most amazing guy and we talk about our future all the time." Sarah L., who has been happily married to Jeff for four years, tells me, "I do not believe 'you know when you know.' I don't think you ever know 100 percent for sure if a guy is the right one for you. I am more of a believer in the 'right for right now' mentality. When Jeff came into my life, he was the right type of guy that I needed. And, fortunately, because steady and reliable is always a good thing, especially for a long-term relationship, he continues to be the right guy for me. However, had I met him in my early twenties when I thrived on drama and excitement, I am not sure we would be together now."

Catherine E. takes a philosophical approach to the notion of "knowing." As she sees in, "To say you 'know' for sure implies a guarantee of some sort. I hate to be pessimistic, but with relationships I don't think it's possible to ever have a true guarantee; if it were that simple, people would never break up or get divorced! I think that you can be 95 percent sure (more or less) and at some point, you have to make that huge leap of faith and decide whether the person is the one you want to be with."

BOTTOM LINE
. . . .

Whether you're talking about the women who "just knew" or those who didn't, one thing is certain: They weren't desperately looking for signs (you don't need to have an "I knew he was The One the moment we kissed" moment) or trying to love a man who wasn't perfect for them. Love takes time, and you have to be willing to let it work its magic.

Chapter Thirteen

Basic Instinct

When Fay met Henry, *she was in her midtwenties and had just come out of a relationship.* "I was in pain and feeling insecure," *she explains.* "He was a rebound for me." *Although there were a couple of things she liked about him, she was far from head over heels.* "There was an acid feeling in my stomach," *she says.* "I thought, You don't like him now, but you will. You will grow to love him. You're fresh off the other relationship, so that's why you can't see him for who he is. When you get over it, you will." *Months passed, and although she managed to get over the breakup, she wasn't entirely sure about Henry. Still, she says,* "I was in a hurry to check off my boxes," *so when he proposed after nine months of dating, she accepted.* "I'd forgotten about my initial gut reaction." *One month before the Big Day, she got cold feet and postponed the nuptials for a year. When the new date rolled around, she says,* "I really didn't want to get married to him then, either. On my wedding day, I thought, Run! Run! But I didn't. I didn't want to admit failure."

Here's something fascinating I learned while researching this book: Studies have shown that one of the areas in our brain affected by love is the same spot that is responsible for our gut feelings, like those butterflies you get when you see your boyfriend—or perhaps, as in Fay's case, the sickness. Columbia University neurobiologist Michael Gershon, M.D., even calls the stomach the "second brain." We're biologically engineered to know when things are right or wrong. This is why you need to trust your instincts when it comes to dating and relationships. "It's the most important thing you can do for yourself," says Dr. Debbie Then. "Really listen to your gut because your stomach doesn't lie."

Thinking about this takes me back to the moment Andrew proposed to me on *The Bachelor*. It was romantic and magical and something I will never forget—but probably not for the reason most people would imagine. In all honesty, when he asked me to marry him, my initial gut reaction wasn't "Woo-hoo!," it was "Whoa." It was panic. Although I'd spent the previous six weeks hoping he'd give me the final rose, and I fantasized about having a relationship with him off the show, the idea of actually marrying him—a guy I really liked but barely knew—freaked me out.

But only for a second.

"Screw you," I told my gut. "This is what I want." So as quickly as it came, the feeling passed and I was back in the excitement of what was going on. I was thrilled that my dream was coming true. I wrote off my first response as a crazy moment. I pretended like it never happened. When Andrew and I got to talking about the future, wedding plans were the furthest thing from our minds. The fact that I had doubts about becoming engaged seemed inconsequential.

Of course, it wasn't. Now, I know that bit of doubt was a (no pun intended) reality check—and the reality was we only knew each other in the context of made-for-TV fantasy dates. It was my instinct telling me this relationship needed to slow down. We needed to get to know each other a lot better before we even could have been serious enough to even think about *thinking about* an engagement. However, I was so thrilled to have been chosen over twenty-four other women that nothing else mattered. My head may not have been in the right place, but, apparently, my gut was. "Women have a built-in radar and know when something doesn't fit," says Then. But there's often one problem (which I think was *my* problem): "They are so in tune to thinking 'Does he like me?' that they often don't think 'Do I like him?' "

ACHES AND PAINS

When I meet a guy I like, I genuinely feel it. I miss him when he's gone. I smile when I talk about him. I get energized when I see his name pop up in my e-mail in-box. Something inside just feels . . . *good.*

And when a relationship isn't working, you can feel

that, too, no matter how much you try to deny it. I always know something isn't right when I don't really care if I see the guy I'm dating. Or if I don't feel sad when he doesn't call. Or if when we're together, things feel strained or out of sync. The problem isn't just that the giddiness is gone (because that's bound to happen even in the best relationships), it's that a sense of anxiety, dread, or even apathy replaces it.

When those uncertain and uneasy feelings set in, *pay attention.* Consider it a sign that it's time to reevaluate your situation. I'm not saying you definitely have to call it quits ("When things get hard, it doesn't mean he or she is not right for you," notes relationship expert Carolyn Bushong), but what's the point in pretending everything is all right? So you can settle?

We let bad relationships continue for a number of reasons: laziness, fear of being single, and concern for the other person's feelings. But another explanation is that, a lot of the time, we don't trust ourselves—we don't trust our guts. Toward the end of more than one relationship I've wondered, What if I'm wrong and I'm giving up something that I shouldn't? But I've never been wrong. I may be single, but I'm happier today than I would have been if I'd stayed with any of my exes. I've learned to stop questioning myself.

It's not even my own experiences that have helped me reach this point. When I hear stories from women like Fay, or my friend Ashley, it only stresses the importance of following your instincts. Ashley, too, had doubts during her engagement and didn't act on them. "I remember fighting with my fiancé and thinking it wasn't 'right,'" she says. "When I told people that I was scared, they chalked it up to prewedding jitters, but I *knew*. I knew the morning of my wedding, I knew the month before, I knew three months before that—and I ignored it." Being in that situation is my worst nightmare.

According to Bushong, "Trusting your gut instincts when your instincts tell you not to do something is usually good; that is, 'I knew he was trouble when I met him.'" However, she warns that you shouldn't equate your gut with a level head. "Women often justify their *own* bad behavior by thinking they're following their instincts; that is, 'It felt so right,' or '. . . but I love him,' when all they are doing is being impulsive and not using their heads to make healthier, smarter decisions," she says. "When we follow our gut in this way, we usually end up regretting what we did."

SHIFTS AND RIFTS

Even the best relationships change over time. It could take months, it could take years, but nothing will ever remain exactly how it was at the beginning. "It's normal to lose that must-have-sex-on-every-surface-of-the-house-twice-a-day passion," says relationship expert Dennie Hughes. "But what should deepen is that feeling of happiness and security, of connection and communication." If you don't have a good, solid foundation, the relationship may crumble. That's why it's so important to really *like* the person you're dating. If all you have is lust, you're in trouble.

As long as you have a deep connection with a man, you will (or at least should) be able to sense in your gut when things start to turn sour. Plenty of women ignore that feeling for way too long, and only end up telling *themselves,* "I told you so." I once dated someone for about a year, and everything started out so perfectly that I even thought we were going to get married. We met right after I came out of a relationship, and I wasn't ready to jump back into another. When I finally came around to him, I fell hard. I thought we were so perfect together that I would have done *anything* for him. But about five months into dating, I felt a shift. Before, he would bend over backward to see me; now, it seemed like he was making me bend over backward to see him. Just when I committed myself to him completely—and forever, in my mind—I sensed he was starting to lose interest. It was as if he was only interested in the chase, and once he realized he had me for good, he didn't want me anymore. At first, I wrote it off as just a bump in the road; however, the sick feeling in my stomach lingered. *Oh no,* I thought. *This isn't going to work out with him.* Quickly, I tried to convince myself everything was fine. I became some kind of robot girl who didn't feel emotions. It didn't help that when I asked my boyfriend how he felt about the relationship he assured me, "I'm fine. I'm happy. We're great." But *I* wasn't great, and I couldn't fool myself any longer. I followed my instinct and broke up with him.

Have enough respect for yourself to at least speak up if you sense something is off in your relationship. "I was going out with a guy for over a year; we were totally in love, and everyone thought we were going to get married," Liza recalls. Even though Paul had a history of commitment problems, she was confident those days were over. "Then, things changed. He started smoking a lot of pot. He wasn't showing up to work. It came to the point where we couldn't relate to each other. He wasn't being kind anymore. He was distant, disengaged, and not being considerate of me, or the relationship." Liza was so bothered that when they were out for dinner one night, she confronted him. "Where is this relationship heading?" she asked. "Something seems to be off with you. What's going on? You're not into work or the relationship. I want to take this to the next level." His response wasn't what she'd expected. "I've been thinking about that, too," he said. "I think we need to break up." After a public meltdown, Paul drove Liza home, where they both cried all night long. "In retrospect, I'm glad I spoke up for myself because the breakup was going to happen eventually," she says. "At least I had control over the situation."

SUCH A DRAG
. . . .

If you don't pay attention to what your gut is telling you, you could end up wasting valuable time. "I dated someone for three and a half years and was probably in it for a year too long," says Melissa. "I would never do that now, but at the time, I was very concerned about hurting him." The pair began dating in college and quickly thought they'd found their soul mate. "But as we grew older and got more settled into our own adult lives, we started wanting different things and becoming different people," she continues. "I was so afraid to tell him that I was having doubts about him being the right person for me in the long term. I thought he would be crushed, so I decided to wait until he was also having doubts. I realize now I should have done what I knew was right as soon as I thought about it."

Helen says her ten-year marriage lasted well past its prime because she just wouldn't accept that everything in her relationship had changed. "I wasn't listening to my instinct," she says. "Over the years, I had changed my way of seeing the world, and it affected what kind of relationship was best for me. Even the people around me could see what I was talking about. It got to the point where I couldn't deny it anymore."

BOTTOM LINE
· ·

Even when you are blinded by love, your gut isn't. If something doesn't feel right, or if you're having doubts about a relationship, say or do something about it. Don't push aside uneasy feelings just for the sake of having a boyfriend.

Chapter Fourteen

. . . .

Your Time Is Precious, Why Waste It?

Last year, I dated a guy who was completely different from me," says Melanie, an LWS. *"Albert and I hardly had anything in common, but we enjoyed each other's company and learning about each other's interests. Still, I knew pretty early on that we weren't compatible, and there were lots of qualities that I would want in my ideal man that this guy didn't have. If I really thought about what my life would be like if I, say, were to marry Albert, it wasn't the life I had pictured for myself. I considered breaking things off. However, he didn't annoy me, as other guys have, and I enjoyed the companionship, so I convinced myself that those things I wanted that he didn't have were superficial and didn't matter. I convinced myself so well, in fact, that when he broke things off, I was extremely hurt. The worst part was feeling like, had I gone with my gut in the beginning, I would have avoided all of this."*

I don't even want to calculate how much of my life I've thrown away on bad relationships. I've stayed with guys because we had the same friends and I didn't want the breakup to affect the group. Another time, I stuck around too long because I was panicked that I wouldn't have anything to do if I was on my own. Who would I spend my weekends with? What if I didn't have plans on a Saturday night? Most recently, I dated a man for three months—two months too long—who, despite being kind, cute, and entertaining, had too many other traits I couldn't handle.

Wouldn't it be nice if we all had crystal balls so we could look into the future and see that we do end up with the men we've been hoping to find? Imagine all of the time we would get to save by not going on bad dates, not having to put up with lame boyfriends, or not having those moments when we worry we might never find The One.

Well, I've decided to act like I already know what happens in my future: I have faith that one day I will end up meeting the perfect guy for me. Therefore, in the meantime, I'm not going to bother dating men I don't absolutely like or those with whom I don't see spending my future. What's the point? Why suffer? We all have so much to offer, there's no reason to waste it on some loser (or even a good guy you just don't like). Your time is much better spent focusing on yourself (something I know one day I'll wish I could do) and cultivating *meaningful* relationships. And sure enough, if you're not wrapped up with the wrong guy, you'll be available when the right one finally does come along.

USERS ARE LOSERS

It's fun to have a regular date on a Saturday night, but the purpose of a boyfriend is not only to fill up your social calendar. Think about it: If you keep someone around just so you have a dinner partner, a movie buddy, or someone to bring to your college roommate's wedding, you might as well just call an escort service. If you're only dating a guy for his physical presence—and not because you actually *want* to be with him—you're essentially using him in the same way.

Three months is the maximum amount of time you should date someone if you're feeling unhappy or unfulfilled. By then, you should know him well enough to figure out if the relationship is worth your time. You don't have to decide if you want to marry him by this point, but if you can't envision a potential future together, you're better off on your own. If you know you want to have kids and that isn't in his plans, find someone else. If you both practice different religions and marrying someone of your faith is essential to either of you, talk about that early on so neither of you wastes time praying for a conversion. The minute you think you don't want to spend the rest of your life (or even the week) with him, get out. Nip bad relationships in the bud before the months become years.

It's easy not to let time slip away if you keep reminding yourself that it's better to be single than sorry. "My life as an independent, single person is just too fun to be

dating someone who gives me reason to pick at them,"
says Melissa. "I mean, seriously, if you are going to
spend your life with this person, they had better not annoy you. I know no one is perfect, but I will have to like
him so much that the little things don't bother me." Re-
tail manager Jacquelyn, 29, also doesn't believe dating
should be a chore. "When you get to a point where
you're staring across the table at him thinking, I'd rather
be at home by myself reading a book than out here on a
Saturday night with you, nothing else matters." However, not every woman agrees. "My one girlfriend would
prefer to at least be out with someone eating a free
meal," adds Jacquelyn. "Life's too short! I want someone
whom I truly enjoy spending time with, and can spend
hours with without even thinking about it." And when
it comes to spending your *life* with a man, we raise our
expectations even higher. As Catherine R. explains,
"Now, there are standards that the men I date have to
meet. It's not just a great guy I'll have a good time with.
If I'm going to begin a monogamous, committed relationship, it should be with a person I'm potentially going to love forever."

STRESS TEST

All couples have their ups and downs, but if the people
who "know" are to be believed, the right relationship
feels effortless. With several of my exes, I'd spend my

days stressing about why we kept arguing, and then I'd forever be dreading the looming breakup. It was exhausting. That's not what love is about. "Love should add to your life," notes relationship expert Sherry Amatenstein.

If you're at all uncertain about your boyfriend, you have to ask yourself some important questions:

- *Is this guy giving me what I want?*
- *Is he making me happy?*
- *Does he make me feel better about myself or worse?*
- *Does he point out my flaws, or do my flaws endear me to him?*
- *Is this who I want to be with on a long-term basis or is he just good enough for now?*
- *Would I be happier without the stress of this person in my life?*

It's hard to be honest with yourself when any of the answers are no. But if you're not gaining anything by being in the relationship, it's not worth your time. My mom always taught me that if you have to ask if you're in love, you're not. You shouldn't have to struggle with it. Relationship expert Dr. Jenn Berman seconds that notion: "If you're nine months into a relationship and think, I don't know if I really like this guy, then you probably don't."

UNPRODUCTIVE BEHAVIOR

On the flip side, don't waste time on someone who isn't into you as much as you are into him. The goal is to love and be loved, not to love and be liked.

It's easy to tell when a relationship is out of balance. Some signs I've picked up from my own experiences: You're the one making all the compromises. You don't feel special or appreciated. You plan your schedule based on his and cater to his every whim—and you know he would never do the same. Both sides of a couple need to work equally to make a relationship successful.

If you find that you have to convince someone to date you, you're wasting your time. Rebecca admits she's tried to talk guys out of breaking up with her on more than one occasion. "I really thought I could change their minds," she says. "A guy would say to me, 'I don't think this is right,' and I kept giving him reasons why we should stay together. Now, I've realized that I was devaluing myself by being with someone who didn't want to be with me."

Another mistake? Spending one single second dating someone who is insulting or disrespectful. It makes me sad and angry when I hear about women who put up with such jerks. Rachel, who recently lost twenty pounds and replaced it with newfound confidence, confesses she used to be one of these doormats. "In the past, I was feeling bad about myself and would have dated anyone," she says. "I stayed with one guy who would treat me so badly. He would tell me I wasn't his type. He would cancel plans. Instead of taking me out for dinner, he would grab a six-pack of beer and we'd go back to his apartment to watch TV. It was humiliating." Another prize she kept around told her she needed to go to finishing school to improve her manners. "I wouldn't do that to myself anymore," she says. "I don't hate myself that much. Even if I'm still not the skinniest person, I feel better so I don't want to settle. It's all about confidence."

You're squandering valuable time—and energy—if you try to justify why a guy seems disinterested in you. If he isn't giving you the attention you deserve, just move on. As married Jamie explains, "I hear single women constantly making up excuses about why a man hasn't pursued them: 'He's been so busy traveling lately" or "He's so shy.' No, he's not into it. Realize it's not really about you and move on to the next dating adventure." Don't hang on to something that isn't there. It only serves to lower your self-esteem. Someone like Dawn has the right attitude: "I'm not desperate," she says. "I don't beg guys. If you don't want to be with me, I don't want to be with you. If you're self-sufficient, there's nothing they can do to hurt you."

FIND YOUR INSPIRATION

I've found that one way to prevent myself from wasting time is by having relationship role models. I know whose relationships I want to emulate—and whose I don't—and

I let that be my guide. Looking at these couples reminds me of what I want, and I won't take anything less for myself. Two rules: Remember that no relationship is perfect, warns says Dr. Berman, and "your role models should be people you actually know, not celebrities."

My own inspiration comes from my friend Lauren and her husband, Bryan. Looking at them, you can just tell they really love each other. They're best friends. They put each other first. They communicate. I've seen them go through the best and worst of times, and they have always stuck together. Catherine R. is similarly moved by her brother and his wife. "They're so goofy and romantic and affectionate," she explains. "I stand back and look at the way they interact and think, They're in love, and they will be in love for the rest of their lives. It's a beautiful, inspiring thing."

My friend Michelle hopes one day she can have a marriage like her parents'. "They do everything together," she says. "I remember when I was growing up, my dad would come home from work, pick up my mom, and they'd just drive to the gas station to fill up the tank. It was their alone time for the evening and the kids couldn't go. I also remember seeing my mother sitting in the bathroom with him while he cleaned up after work, just talking about the day." Relationship expert Dennie Hughes tells me that she's picked her mom and dad, too. "They've been married for forty-five years," she says. "He always reaches for her hand when they walk together. He always notices when she's wearing something new. Sometimes, when they're in the kitchen together, she'll grab him and they'll dance. They never fight disrespectfully and they never go to bed mad."

Your role model doesn't even have to be a couple. Rachel's is a single coworker. "A lot of her friends are married and have babies, but she never panics or seems bitter," she explains. "I've never heard her complain about not having a boyfriend for Valentine's Day. When she met someone, I thought, This person is really deserving. I don't think she's settled."

BOTTOM LINE

Know what kind of relationship you want and don't accept anything less. Value yourself, your time—and your life. Breakups are never easy, but when I end a bad relationship, I always feel like a weight has been lifted. I'm less worried, less stressed. I can relax and be excited about the future—and a relationship I deserve. Anything else is a waste of time.

Part Five

♥

Compromise, Yes;
Settle, No

Chapter Fifteen

· · · · · · · · · · · · · · · · ·

Are You Still There?

*T*here was a time *when I didn't have such great self-esteem and I used to turn myself into whatever the man I was with wanted," says Dawn. "My ex-boyfriend Steve was a total Harley-Davidson guy. I'm terrified of motorcycles, but I would get on his bike all the time. I also started dressing like a biker chick, wearing tank tops and chokers—it was so not me. My friends even noticed and made comments." With another boy-friend, she found herself immersed in the world of muscle cars. "Again, not my thing," she says, "but I would go to events with him, and we'd watch NASCAR racing on Saturday mornings. I wanted to slash my wrists." Now that she's more confident and isn't afraid to be single, her days of being a dating chameleon are over. "I would never do that again," she swears. "I wouldn't sit there and pretend to be into things I didn't like. I'd get up and go shopping and meet the guy later."*

According to one survey, 58 percent of people admit they have changed who they are to get the approval of their partner. Every relationship requires a certain level of compromise, but completely altering your style, interests, personality, and/or core beliefs for someone is not what it's about. I mean, look at Katie Holmes. She's a prime example of how not to behave in a relationship. When she started dating Tom Cruise, she gave up her entire life to fit into his: She adopted his religion, copied his mannerisms, and reportedly dropped her friends. I feel incredibly sorry for her. It's as if she's become a lifeless creature who is simply going through the motions. When you're in a relationship, no one should ever have to wonder, "Are you still there?"

To be fair, it's natural to expect some level of change when you're part of a couple; when two people grow close, their personalities and interests are bound to rub off on each other. Some transformation even can be good—say, if a man's influence makes you more generous or punctual. But I speak from experience when I say sacrificing your identity for the sake of another person is a huge mistake. After *The Bachelor* I was so intent on making my relationship with Andrew a success that I made every aspect of my life revolve around his: I moved to *his* city, lived in *his* apartment with *his* roommate and worked for *his* family's company. To make matters worse, I was always worried about doing anything that would reflect badly on the Firestone family, so I felt like I had to be on my guard all of the time. I didn't let the real me show through.

You'd think I would have learned my lesson, but in

my first post-*Bachelorette* relationship, with a nightlife entrepreneur, I once again adapted my life and my personality to suit his. Due to the nature of his career, he spends basically every night on the town, mingling and schmoozing. I don't love going out *all* the time, and I don't have the energy (or desire) to be "on" at every moment. But that's what I did when I was with him because that's what *he* did, and I wanted us to be together. (It's so easy to fall into this trap because you think you're being a good girlfriend.) It was physically and emotionally taxing. I yearned to sit at home and watch a movie, but it just wasn't possible. Eventually, I ended up resenting him because I felt like I was doing everything to accommodate him, and he wasn't as flexible. As my mom has always told me, relationships take work and you have to be willing to compromise for the other person—but hopefully you're getting just as much in return. If you're not, it's not worth it.

A man should love you for who you are, or, as *Sex and the City*'s Carrie Bradshaw so perfectly put it, he should "love the you that you love." (That's why people in great relationships say it's so easy: They don't have to try so hard to make it work.) Pretending you're someone else will only lead to trouble. For one thing, warns relationship expert Dennie Hughes, transforming into the "perfect" woman can leave a guy bored. "Once she becomes the Stepford model, he loses interest and moves on to the next conquest," she explains. And that says nothing about what it will do to you. When I've changed for someone, I've felt depressed, miserable, and lonely. (Though I was part of a couple, I wasn't even there to keep myself company.) At some point, the real you will want to come out, and then there's no guarantee the guy is even going to like her.

You need to have enough respect for yourself to know when you're compromising your identity. As Dr. Jenn Berman explains, "The sign that it's too much change is when you're giving up yourself in order to accommodate your partner's hobbies and interests and life. When it becomes all about him and not at all about you, you're in trouble."

IMPERFECT FIT

Changing too much for a man and settling often go hand in hand. Desperation, after all, is one of the reasons why a woman would even entertain the idea of altering her persona for a guy. She meets someone who seems ideal, and tries to fit the mold of the kind of person she thinks he wants. It doesn't matter that he might not be the right man for her so long as she's willing to make herself the right woman for him. Nikki, a 28-year-old sales executive, is a similar case. When she began dating Marty, a well-to-do politician, she ditched her pop music CDs, toned down her extroverted personality, and started dressing conservatively. "She used to be such a silly and fun person," says her friend Corinne. "Now, she tries to be so proper. Her old self only comes out when Marty's not around. It's so sad." Valerie admits she became another woman during her failed engagement. "When I was with my fiancé, I lost a bit of the independent, wild-child flirty girl," she says. "I missed her."

Face the fact: If you can't be yourself around a man—no matter how great he is—*he is not the right one for you*. The person you are when you're single should be essentially the person you are when you're in a couple (although perhaps a bit less selfish, and certainly less boy-crazy).

SHAPE-SHIFTING

It's amazing—and funny and sad—what women are willing to do for the sake of a relationship. Carly readily admits she's started wearing sweatsuits because they're her boyfriend's wardrobe staple. "My sister keeps saying, 'Why are you trying to dress like him?' But he made this point about how much more comfortable sweats are," she explains. Carly says that when she scoffed at the idea, he wanted to know who she was trying to impress. She couldn't give him a valid answer. The result? "I wear a lot more sweatsuits now."

In contrast, I once had a boyfriend who wanted me to dress more provocatively. He'd even send me out on shopping trips with one of his scantily clad female friends. When I'd come back with short skirts and cleavage-baring tops he'd hug, kiss, and thank his friend.

But almost every time I tried to dress to please him, I'd change out of the outfit before I even left the bedroom. It just wasn't me.

Natalie, who used to hate to cook, says she tried to become Betty Crocker while she was dating "a country boy" in college. "I tried to mimic what he might want. It didn't work out." Joanie confesses she altered her wardrobe per a request from her ex-husband. "I tried to be less 'trendy,'" she says. "That was his word. I was too up-market for his family!" Even worse, she dumbed herself down to fit in with his friends. "I even used to 'throw' family games of Trivial Pursuit because they'd get angry that I knew too many answers," she adds. "I went from being a funny, smart woman to a quiet, somewhat introverted one. It was a nightmare."

Keeping up a facade is never easy. When Gerard e-mailed Paula after a one-year gap with news that he was single again, she thought it was a chance for them to get back together. She was so eager to show him that she was stronger and more confident than she'd been when they dated. Although that was true, she decided it needed to be extra noticeable. "I tried to act very composed and together," she says. "I wanted him to see that I've changed." At the time, she told a friend, "I don't think I can pull it off for too long." And she couldn't. After spending a nice, nonromantic weekend together, she cracked, and the old, insecure Paula resurfaced. "Aren't you going to kiss me?!" she asked Gerard just before he drove her home. He didn't even answer; Paula was mortified. Not only was there no kiss, but he also didn't even make a follow-up phone call to recap the weekend. Paula's dream of rekindling the flame was dashed.

What determines if a change will stick? The motivation behind it. Jacquelyn told me about a former relationship in which she and her boyfriend were constantly trying to make each other into different people. "It just ended up in resentment and big arguments," she says. A major issue: sports. "He'd always try to get me to go Rollerblading or running with him, but I hated it," she says. "I just ended up disliking that part of him and avoided sports altogether." Ironically, once they broke up and he wasn't pressuring her to become an athlete, she developed a passion for running. "Probably all that nagging made me think about it and do something about it," she says, "but I never would have maintained it had I done it for him. I changed because I wanted to change for myself."

DISAPPEARING ACTS

Male or female, if you want to preserve your identity while you're in a relationship, you have to stay in touch with your friends. They're the ones who remind you who you are and will call you out if they see you change too much (just like Dawn's friends did when she went all biker chick). Being "still there" doesn't only have to do with your personality, it also involves your physical presence. It's pathetic when anyone pulls a disappearing act on their friends just because they're in a relationship. "I dated a guy for four years, and I went through a time when I ditched my friends to be with him and do everything for him, even his laundry," says Natalie. "I was blinded by the idea of being in love. Now, I look back at that person and I'm embarrassed that I was ever *her*. In my current relationship, I'm very conscious of my actions, and I'm also much more secure."

While I can appreciate wanting to spend every waking moment with the man you adore, I've never lost sight of the fact that my life is made up of a number of people, not just one. You shouldn't be so involved with a man that no one else matters anymore. Even when I'm part of a couple, I still make time for all of the things that were important to me before we met. I still need to shop, gossip, and talk about who does my hair for an hour—things I can't do with a man. "Your boyfriend or husband will have to be a big shoulder to cry on, but nine out of ten times he won't know what to say because he's a guy!" notes Elizabeth. Everyone needs a support system outside of a relationship; otherwise you become one of those annoyingly needy and clingy girlfriends. It's a role so many women (myself included) take pains to avoid. "I never want to be the type that ditches all her friends when she gets a boyfriend," says Lea. "I'll make a point to plan lots of activities with girlfriends—walks, TV nights—and stick to them. Everyone needs time away from their significant others in order to have a healthy relationship."

When I first moved in with Andrew, I inadvertently lost touch with people because I was so wrapped up in working, attending events for his family's winery, post-*Bachelor* interviews, photo shoots, and making red carpet appearances. (Poor me, I know.) I felt so far away from my world in Chicago, and my friends there just couldn't comprehend what was really going on in my life—and, for that matter, neither could I. After about a month, I finally got my bearings and was able to reconnect with everyone I'd left behind. I even made frequent trips back home just so they (and I) knew I wasn't out of the picture for good.

Finding a way to give everyone the attention they deserve can be tricky, but it's worth it. For one, if you cut off all contact, no one will be around to accept a tearful call after a fight or a breakup. "It takes some juggling and understanding," says Francine, "and a guy who doesn't insist on being attached at the hip all the time." Needless to say, any guy who *keeps* you from being with your friends is not worth your time.

BIG DECISIONS

As passionately as I feel about not changing for another person, I can't ignore the fact that there are times when you may be forced to choose between your honey and your life. For example, what happens when you're in an interfaith relationship? What happens when you and your guy live in separate cities? What about when you don't agree on topics such as marriage or kids? How do you determine which is more important: your own identity or your relationship?

There's never a perfect answer; in the end, something (and someone) has got to give. While you have to be able to adapt to situations, you should think long and hard—and then even longer and harder—before you relinquish an important part of your life for a man. You have to be 100 percent okay with your decision; otherwise, you're settling. You may be part of a couple, but it's your life, too. You can't *only* be doing it for the guy—you have to remember to think about yourself, and be okay with your choices *on your own*. According to relationship expert Sherry Amatenstein, "Things should be a *compromise*, not a sacrifice." And naturally, you have to be sure the guy is worth the trade-off. "No one should ever make these kinds of life decisions without knowing that the relationship is solid, and long term and committed," adds Hughes.

One of my biggest regrets is that I gave up my life in Chicago too quickly to be with Andrew. I've always wondered what would have happened (or if things would have turned out differently) if I had given myself a little more time to sort everything out. At the time, though, I felt like I didn't have a choice. Since he couldn't move to Chicago or carry on a long-distance relationship (his work schedule wouldn't allow it), it was up to me to decide if our relationship was going to continue. I didn't want to leave everything I knew, but I also wasn't ready to leave our relationship behind. Because I was so swept up in the postshow excitement, I felt like I *had* to be with Andrew—and fast. I never stopped to think about what life would be like with nothing familiar around and nothing to call my own. I would have saved a lot of tears if I had taken my time moving, looked into career opportunities, and, most important, made my decision for myself, not just my boyfriend (who, let's not forget, I'd only known for a matter of months).

A relationship can't be one-sided. If somebody really cares about you, he'll want what's best for both of you, not just himself. We should all be as lucky as Sarah M.: A few months before she graduated from college, her boyfriend (now husband), Chris, already had a job and was settled in Long Island, renting an apartment. "I had plans of my own," she says. "I wanted to live in New York City for a year or two before we made any permanent decisions. Chris was completely supportive of this and suffered through two years of me living two hours away. He knew how much it meant to me to be on my own. He never pressured me to move or leave my job. If he had, I think it would have been a deal breaker."

That's almost what happened with Clare, who had a hard time reconciling her feminist side with the side of herself that was willing to relocate for her boyfriend while he finished graduate school. "I was fiercely independent and would not bend to the will of a significant other," she says. "I held on to the notion that if I moved to Boston to be with him, then I would be giving up my independence, and that the move, in and of itself, would actually change what type of person I was." Eventually, she realized she was overthinking the situation. "The reality was, if I moved to Boston, and it was *my* choice—which, in the end, it has to be—then I wouldn't have changed as fundamentally as I had feared that I would. I was still dictating what happened with my life, not him. Plus, on my list of priorities, my happiness had to rank the highest. When I realized that I was happiest living with my best friend—as he turned out to be—how could I think of denying that to myself? It ended up being the logical choice, no matter how difficult."

Jodi S. relocated from New York City to London to be with her English boyfriend, something she never imagined she'd do for anyone. "I'm an extremely independent person and was very used to being on my own," she says. "Sometimes, though, you just have to take a chance." The couple dated long distance for two years, all the while getting to know each other over the phone. "We had long, drawn-out, frustrating conversations about moving that ended up going nowhere," she recalls. "It was to the point where I would cover my ears as I just couldn't stand it anymore." Jodi's boyfriend considered moving, but due to U.S. immigration issues, it was too difficult. Jodi, however, was able to transfer within her company. "That essentially made the decision for us," she explains. Although she admits she was homesick and resentful at first, she's growing to love her new life. "I'm becoming more independent as time goes on and know eventually I'll feel as comfortable as I did back home," she says. "All in all, I have to say it was worth it. I think the main factor in my decision was that he was the first person I've been with who has accepted and loved every quirk, flaw, etc., without condition and I feel the same. Having to give up my job, apartment, family, and friends was an enormous sacrifice, but I know he would do the same for me in an instant."

BOTTOM LINE

There's no doubt you're going to transform when you're in a relationship, but it should never be so much that the person you were when you were single disappears. You shouldn't have to alter your personality (or wardrobe or anything else) just to please a man. Anytime you make a change, make sure you're doing it for yourself.

Chapter Sixteen

What You Want Versus
What You Need

A few years ago at a wine-tasting party, Melissa was chatting with a married female guest. "She asked me whether I was dating anyone, and I wasn't, so she asked me what I was looking for in a man," she recalls. "I told her I didn't really know. What she said after that really stuck with me: 'How will you be able to find anyone if you don't know what you're looking for?' " Later that week, Melissa decided to figure it out. "I actually wrote out a list of things that I am looking for—qualities and traits that I really want in a husband. Eleven of them, to be exact. The list is stored in the 'Projects' section of my day planner. If anything, it reminds me of what I eventually want, so as I'm dating guys and figuring out who they are, I won't settle on any characteristic that is undesirable to me. And I won't settle for someone who is missing something big."

Not everyone is as organized as Melissa, but we all have lists, at least floating around in our heads, describing the type of guy and relationship we want. I don't even know how old (or young) I was when I started compiling mine, but it's constantly growing and changing. For instance, when I saw *Sixteen Candles,* I decided I wanted a guy who drove a red Porsche like Jake Ryan—and looked like him, too. After *Dirty Dancing,* I added that he would have to someday come to my rescue and say, "Nobody puts Jennifer in a corner."

Fortunately, as I began dating and matured, my desires became more realistic. I also realized some of the things I used to consider major—such as hair color—are less important than others, like respect. These days, my list is split into two categories: wants and needs. These lists help me establish my priorities and remind me what I aspire for in my life. They're based as much on my former relationships as they are on my periods of being single. After all, the best time to get to know yourself is when you're on your own.

My list is my ticket to not settling. I've seen so many women toss theirs aside because they're feeling desperate. For example, just two weeks after Paula ended things with a past boyfriend because they weren't members of the same religion—one of her absolute needs—she started seeing him again because a relationship with a man she liked more didn't work out. "Well, he seems like he may not be committed to his religion," she told a friend. Mind you, they didn't have a conversation about him converting; this was just something she was telling herself because she craved a boyfriend.

As a rule, it's okay to let go of some of your wants, but never your needs. "Needs are deal breakers," explains psychotherapist Dr. Jenn Berman. "If you don't get them in your relationship, then the relationship isn't for you." I'm not saying you should only be with men who meet every one of your criteria (the luckiest woman in the world probably couldn't find someone like that), but if you back down on the things that are *most* important to you, you're settling. "If you give up everything, I don't know what you get," notes Liza.

MAKING LISTS

Figuring out the difference between your wants and needs isn't always easy. In many cases, you have to make trade-offs. For example, most women yearn for a man who is very successful, but that often means not being able to spend a lot of time together. You have to ask yourself, What's more important, the Lexus (and being lonely) or the Jetta (and companionship)? There is no right or wrong answer; it's whatever works for you—and that's something you may not even be able to figure out until you're in a relationship. "I only realized what I needed to make me happy once I found it," admits Rebecca. "I had to walk into it." What was it that

she discovered she needed? "Someone who was unconditionally devoted to me. I didn't have to convince him
to be with me or sell myself or make myself something
I wasn't."

Of course, you can't just sit around waiting for your
needs to reveal themselves. If you're bored one day and
want a productive way to pass the time instead of surfing the Web for the latest celebrity gossip, make a Love
List. Use a pencil to jot down your wants, and a pen for
your needs (because, if anything, you should be adding
to those, never subtracting). Think about your relationship likes and dislikes and write them down, too. According to relationship expert Dennie Hughes, a few
things are required to appear on every woman's list.
"You need a guy who is honest, respectful and loyal and
makes you a priority."

Lea once compiled a list about what she wants in a
husband while instant messaging with her mother. She
has it saved on her computer and shared it with me.

> *MOM11742: Make your list of requirements!*
> *Lea1: Ok, I have them down.*
> *MOM11742: What are they?*
> *Lea1:*
> ❖ *needs to be taller than me*
> ❖ *needs to own a suit*
> ❖ *good sense of humor, thoughtful,*
> *ambitious*

+ *no drinking or anger issues*
+ *physically attractive*
+ *good in social situations*
+ *good in-law situation*
+ *good table manners/polite in general*
+ *good grammar*
+ *ambitious*

Lea1: For starters

You don't have to show your list to anyone, but don't throw it away, either. It's important to glance at it every once in a while to remind yourself of your goals. When you're dating someone, especially if you're unsure about the guy, compare your reality to your wishes. You can also use the list to keep yourself in check; you should never be changing your requirement just to suit a man. They come first, he follows. By having everything written down, you won't waste time in a bad relationship. If you see right in front of you that you're not getting what you want and need—there has to be a lot more good than bad—it's time to make changes or move on.

As I've mentioned, I've broken up with men because they didn't put me before the rest of their lives. One of my exes, in fact, scheduled an out-of-town business meeting on my birthday one year. It wasn't something he had to do on that specific date, but he did it anyway. To make up for being away, he gave me diamond earrings. Do I *want* to be showered in jewels? Sure. But I *need* to be showered in attention.

What are some of my other necessities? Here's a portion of my list:

Wants	Needs
✦ Good style	✦ Good character
✦ Nice voice, a full head of hair, six feet tall, manly hands, fit body	✦ Chemistry
✦ He puts the toilet seat down	✦ He doesn't put me down
✦ A man who likes to have a good time	✦ A man who enjoys being with me
✦ A vacation home	✦ A loving home

I realize some of my wants are superficial—and there's nothing wrong with that. Honestly, if I didn't get absolutely everything in the left-hand column, I'd still be happy. What's more important to me is that I have someone I can talk to, relate to, and laugh with when something great happens. I need to be with a man who is funny, considerate, and trustworthy. I need him to listen to what I have to say. I need him to accept me for who I am, weird reality TV past and all. It may annoy me that he doesn't pick up his socks, but I'd be able to deal with it as long as he's there for me emotionally and picks me up when I'm down.

ADJUSTING PRIORITIES

Since I've reached an age when I'm looking for a long-term relationship, the items on my list reflect that. Back when I was 22 and out for a good time, pretty much all I needed was I guy I found attractive. Now, I look at his values and what he's accomplished in his life. I'm more of an adult, and more adult things matter. As Amy puts it, "I look at what my life is going to be like in twenty years and what will be important then, and it's easier to sort out the must-haves versus the would-likes," she says.

Still, the past is as influential as the future. "The more dating experience you have, the more likely you are to have clarity about what you really need," says Berman. "A lot of women have misconceptions—'I just need a rich man, I just need a man who does this and that. I just need a man who is the same religion as me.' But the truth is, relationships are much more complicated than that. And in order for you to know who the right person for you is, you have to have a lot of confidence in who you are. Most women who are very young don't know a lot about themselves. The more experience you have under your belt, the more capable you are of making a great relationship."

Over the years, Dawn's list has grown to include

"generosity," something she didn't always think about. "Not monetary generosity," she explains, "but someone caring about my happiness. I believe that relationships that work are the ones where each person puts the other partner's happiness first. I want everything that they want." Annie admits she has become pickier over the years, but it's because she's looking for an ideal companion. "I used to hit on the hottest guy in the room," she says. "Now I want to know if they have a job and a passport. I also want someone who can hold a conversation and make me laugh. I don't want someone with road rage, someone with a BMW and a sh—ty apartment, or someone who thinks they are smarter than me because I am a girl. Also a big no-no? Someone who has big ideas but never follows through with any of them."

Going through a divorce helped Valerie gain perspective on her needs. "I came up with this whole theory of Rs," she explains. "All of these things have to be present to have a successful marriage or relationship: romance, respect, religion, reality—like a reality check." After Ashley's marriage ended, she whittled her list down to one bare essential. "I need, I absolutely need to be with someone who is just as nuts for me as I am for him," she told me via e-mail. "I need to be with someone I am passionate about, not someone who merely meets my checklist of requirements. Let's face it, there are a million guys who fulfill the basics: He makes you laugh, earns a good living, smart, blah, blah, blah, *but,* for me, it's the chemistry that matters."

KEEP YOUR OPTIONS OPEN

A big mistake so many women make is thinking they only want to be with one kind of man. I'm not talking about a thoughtful, caring, smart, successful, funny guy—that's a given. What I mean is the tall guy, or the brown-haired guy, or the one who hails from a certain part of the country. You have to leave open the possibility that the man who might fulfill your needs might not look, act, or be affiliated with the political party you always imagined. "The more narrow the parameters, the less likely the chances are of finding love," warns relationship expert Sherry Amatenstein.

Of course, I'm not advocating pursuing a relationship with someone when there's no chemistry. As I've said, that's settling. What I'm talking about is what happens when you find chemistry (and a whole bunch of other necessities) with someone you never pictured as your ideal. Don't be stupid and throw that away because he's not the kind of guy with whom you imagined yourself. I saw this happen with my friend Mandy. She always thought she wanted to be married to a man who made enough money so she could stay home with the children and not have to work. Her boyfriend, Barry, however, makes less than she does. But she's realized that he gives her so much in terms of love and friendship (needs that weren't being met by her asshole ex-boyfriend) that she wouldn't trade him for anyone in the world.

I was surprised by how many women told me their

boyfriends and husbands were nothing like the men they'd imagined they would be. Carly, who hates dance clubs and gym rats, is seriously dating a techno-loving bodybuilder. Liza had a history of going after motorcycle-riding musicians who chain-smoked, did drugs, and were, as she puts it, "total badasses who didn't want me." She married Jack, a kind, considerate, slightly odd, metrosexual banker. "Maybe I just grew up," she explains. "I just liked being with him so much and our relationship evolved naturally." After several failed relationships, Sarah D. says she consciously decided to go after a different kind of man. "As a result," she says, "I finally agreed to go out with the WASPy finance boy who'd been pursuing me for months, and now we're in love."

Daniele, who says her type was always "big, athletic alpha male types" (one of her exes was a six-foot-eight college basketball player), is married to a six-foot-tall man who performed professionally in musical theater between college and law school. "He didn't really fit the mold, but I think it's because I had the wrong idea about the type of person who would be the best partner for me," she says. That's certainly what happened in Sarah L.'s case. "I was always in relationships that were very passionate, full of highs and lows. We either adored each other or hated each other. I think I thrived more on the drama than I did on the actual guy," she admits. "My husband, Jeff, is steady and reliable—not the type of guy I thought I would end up with. There weren't any games. I could just be myself. Jeff is the opposite of me and we balance each other. But of course, we are on the same page with the really important stuff, which makes being together work."

When Liz tried online dating before she met her husband, she always expressed that she was looking for a guy who enjoyed going to bars. "My husband is a teetotaler," she says. "You should have ideals you hold close to your heart, that you could never compromise on. The rest, you just never know. The more open-minded you are, the better off you'll be." Indeed, high school administrator Jessie, 33, was always in search of someone who was from New York City, but not living there—just like herself. She was also looking for someone who shared her interests, values, and liberal political beliefs. Physically, she pictured him having rugged good looks. As she explains, "I didn't go around saying I wanted to find a fair-skinned, balding, red-haired Republican from Arizona—which is who I married."

Katherine confesses, "I always thought that I was going to wind up with the perfect guy who had the perfect job, the perfect friends, the perfect family, and this life where things just came easily. You know what? All of those details that you thought would be so important get thrown out the door when you fall in love. I make almost four times more than my boyfriend, and I am three years younger! He comes from a divorced family; my parents have been happily married for thirty-five years. I come from an upper-middle-class family; he comes from a working-class family. He drives a beat-up

Toyota truck; I drive a Saab. He wears ugly jeans and he snores so badly we often wake up in different rooms! But for all the right reasons, we are madly in love. All that other stuff just doesn't matter anymore. He's funny, smart, thoughtful, witty, adventurous, adorable, respectful, loving, and most of all, treats me as if there is no other woman on earth that could be better. He is amazing and in my eyes, I got the better end of the bargain. You have to realize that the Prince Charming you are looking for could be in anyone."

On the other hand, the man you always thought would be your prince could turn into a frog. Sometimes, even when you think you're with your ideal man, the relationship doesn't work out. "I had the fairy tale," says Valerie. "I didn't have to work, I had a home, a European car, a dog. I had a plane, for God's sake. I had everything, but those were all material things. And I had a guy who loved me very much, but he was weak. And it was the kind of weak that I couldn't live with."

Recently divorced Helen tells me, "I thought Stefan was my ideal; otherwise I wouldn't have gotten married to him. He is someone of such great intelligence. I could ask him any question—about underwater welding, or the economic structure of China—and he could answer it. He's such a funny person. He still makes me laugh. And he's such a good-looking guy, too." After being together for ten years, what went wrong? "I changed," she says. "So then my ideal changed. We could have been married until we died, but I changed so much that there was no way he could stay on the same level."

Let's face it, no matter how organized and goal oriented we are, some things will always be out of our control.

LITTLE ISSUES, BIG PROBLEMS

Don't confuse your idiosyncrasies with your true wants and needs. I was in a relationship once where my boyfriend and I used to fight because I found it annoying that he would get up to empty the dishwasher as soon as the cycle was done. For some reason, it made me nuts. As he was taking out the plates, I would stare at him and wonder if I could ever marry him and put up with this for a lifetime. I would try to tell myself that it wasn't a big deal, but I couldn't get over it. What I finally realized was that he just wasn't right for me—anal behavior or not. Afterward, I didn't add "must not engage in prompt unloading" to my list of wants or needs, because I know that if the right guy came along and he had the same habit, I'd probably help him put away the dishes. Says Ashley, "When you don't have chemistry, the way someone eats their peas can drive you nuts, and when you are crazy about somebody, you just don't feel that way. You think it's endearing."

If insignificant things are driving you crazy, there's probably an underlying cause. My friend Shelly would

get mad when her boyfriend wouldn't clean up the bathroom when she asked. I can understand how if you're a
neat freak and the person you're with isn't, that can be
difficult. But the relationship shouldn't end because the
lotion isn't being put away. Nor should it be the end of
the world if a guy leaves the toilet seat up. It really an-
noys me when I hear women complain about that. Get
over it. It's certainly a nice gesture, but if he fails to do
that, it doesn't mean he doesn't love you. When a relationship is working and I'm getting everything I need
(and most of what I want), I don't sweat the small stuff.
All of the good things outweigh the little day-to-day
annoyances.

An older friend once told me that as time passes, you
become more open-minded and willing to accept men
who fulfill fewer requirements on your list. Instead of
saying, "I need him to meet all ten," you're happy with
seven or eight. How is this not settling? Because she
was only talking about letting go of the little things.
"There is something about still maintaining standards,
and not sweating the small stuff," says Sarah B. "When
I was dating, it wouldn't be that unusual for me to meet
a divorced guy, for example. Was that my ideal situation? No, but it happens. And I realized it's more important to be with someone good than just someone
who doesn't have 'marks against him.' Things like balding, a couple of extra pounds, back hair—all that stuff is
so unimportant." Adds Lea, "Everyone has quirks and
annoying habits. You need to look at the big picture

and determine your threshold for dealing with some of these issues. Some things you need to be able to 'let go' if you really like the person."

BOTTOM LINE

Once again, it all comes back to trusting your gut. If you're getting most of what you want and all of what you need from someone, the relationship will feel right. Don't ever let a man tell you you're too needy. If he isn't providing what you need to be happy, he's not the guy for you.

Chapter Seventeen

Make Demands

Jennifer and Adam, both 32, were dating long distance for more than a year when they decided she would relocate from New York City to Boston so they could be together. Although Jennifer was excited, her parents were not. "They were very against me moving in with a man I was not, at the very least, engaged to," she explains. "I had to defend my relationship and myself over and over again." Several months passed (she was taking her time leaving NYC) and they continued to disapprove. "By the time the summer came, I was tired of fighting with my family," she recalls. "I thought I shouldn't be the only one taking the heat, so I said to Adam, 'You want me to move to Boston? Put on some gloves and get in the ring, buddy. Tell my parents you're not going to get me up there and break my heart in two. You want me, you fight for me.'" What ended up happening? "I joke now that he was too scared to have that conversation, so he asked them if he could marry me instead," she says. "In the end we had everyone's blessing, and I had this beautiful ring."

See what can happen when you speak up for yourself? Certainly not every demand you make is going to score you a marriage proposal, but if you're not getting what you want or need, your happiness depends on saying something about it.

Most people might think of me as a quiet, easygoing person, but when it comes to my relationships, I don't suffer in silence. If I'm feeling neglected, I ask for more attention. If I really want my boyfriend to join me at an event, I'll tell him how important it is to me. If I don't think he's listening to me, I will point it out. I don't expect to get *everything* I ask for (sometimes, just being heard and understood is enough), but the least I can do is make him aware of my feelings.

Among the things you should demand from the man in your life are respect, honesty, and compromise. And when I say demand, I don't mean act like a nagging bitch until you get what you want. I simply mean be vocal and be firm. So many confident and independent single women turn into pushovers when they're in relationships. A lot of that behavior stems from a fear of losing the guy. However, if you don't make demands, you could end up losing *yourself.*

In May 2006, I read an amazing article in *Glamour* magazine written by Kristin Armstrong (ex-wife of cyclist Lance Armstrong) in which she admitted she did just that during her relationship. Now, her hope is to prevent the same thing from happening to other women. She wrote, "Marriage has the potential to erode the very fiber of your identity. If you aren't careful, it can tempt you to become a 'yes woman' for the sake of salvaging your romantic dream. It can lure you into a pattern of pleasing that will turn you into someone you'll hardly recognize and probably won't like."

Even if you're in the initial stages of dating, you shouldn't waste time silently hoping a guy will change a behavior you don't like, or wishing he'd do something he hasn't done. How is he even supposed to know you're having issues if you don't tell him? Men are not mind readers. Communication is one of the most essential components of any relationship. Don't be afraid to make yourself—and your wants and needs—heard. As Armstrong wrote, "If you need help, raise your hand and jump up and down."

BACK IT UP

The reason I'm so forthright with my boyfriends is because I've learned from my mistakes. One relationship in particular taught me that not only is it important to speak up, but it's just as critical to back up what you demand. That means, if you say, "I need you to do X for me," and he doesn't follow through, there have to be consequences. In other words, you can't make threats that you're not going to keep. If you say you're going to leave, you can't just walk toward the door with the hopes that he'll beg you to stay. (I used to do this all the time in the heat of an argument and never once did any boyfriend try to keep me from going. So then, even more pissed off that he didn't come after me, I would walk back inside having just one more thing to fight about. I just looked silly and passive-aggressive; it's all very embarrassing.)

Near the end of our relationship, I kept telling my ex I needed to spend some quality alone time with him, and when I didn't see him making any effort to be with me, I would foolishly give him more chances and listen to excuses like, "I have so much going on right now and I'm trying to fit you in as best as I can." Fit me in? I don't want to be fit into someone's schedule. I am busy, too, but I make time because I want to, not because I need to. I want to be a priority, not an appointment. I should have known after two months the relationship wasn't going to work, but I let it go on for a year. To be more precise, I let him walk all over me for a year. What I should have done was either learn to accept his behavior (instead of letting it continuously bother me) or get out when I realized nothing was going to change. Thinking about it still makes be angry, and we've been broken up for years.

Holding in your feelings can only lead to future resentment. The earlier you start speaking up, the more solid of a foundation you will create. "The beginning of a marriage is a lot easier when you have already duked it out," explains Sarah B. "That's when all the adjustments, learning, and prioritization needs to happen. We girls shouldn't be too scared to rock the boat and demand what we need. As my husband says, I gave him the chippity-chop three or four times while we were dating. Those arguments and negotiations helped us to get to an even ground."

Making demands is simply a sign of self-respect. If you don't create boundaries and speak your mind when you're upset, that only sets a bad precedent for the rest of the relationship. "My biggest lesson was I didn't hold my boundaries," says Fay, who, as you'll recall, stayed with her husband even though he cheated on her four times. "I tried to accommodate a lot. There is accommodation in a relationship, but not when you're trespassing on who you are."

THE PRESSURE PROBLEM

As much as I believe in demands, I'm not a fan of ultimatums. If a man is under extreme pressure to do something—usually, it's to propose—how can you be sure his intentions are genuine and not just a result of stress and fear? It reminds me of a story I heard about a couple, Susannah and James. They had been dating for five years and seemed to be on track to marry. When James was offered a job overseas, Susannah told him the only way she'd go was with a ring on her finger. He dragged his feet, even went on a two-month solo soul-searching trip around the world, and then finally popped the question. A wedding date was set before they relocated. But just a few months into their new life, James had second thoughts (or maybe it was more like his first thought): He wasn't ready to get married. They broke up. I can understand wanting a clear commitment if you're packing up your life for a man, but an engagement (as I've learned) is no guarantee that a relationship will work.

My friend Caroline, 29, had lived with her boyfriend for five years before he planned to head to an out-of-state graduate school. They had spoken about marriage in the past, but she didn't know if he planned on getting engaged before or after he earned his degree. Either way, it was assumed that she'd move with him. However, she was concerned: What if she helped support him through school, and then he ended up breaking up with her? She seriously considered drawing up a document that said he'd pay her back if they broke up. Sounds extreme, but she didn't want to give an ultimatum or force him into marrying her out of guilt. Luckily, he proposed before they left.

If you give an ultimatum, you have to be willing to deal with the consequences you're offering. "If you issue one and back off," warns relationship expert Dennie Hughes, "he will never, ever believe you again." They don't always work, either. Amy once told an ex-boyfriend he needed to choose between her or his friends. "I stuck with it," she says. "It blew up in my face. Bastard." However, as Elizabeth learned, not getting what you want isn't always a bad thing. "I told an ex that either he needed to figure himself out and change or I was moving on," she recalls. "I stuck to it and moved on with my life. Best thing I ever did."

Carly found herself in an interesting predicament when her boyfriend told her he wasn't sure if he ever wants to get married. "The question isn't whether he wants to commit to me," she explains, "it's what 'marriage' has to do with a commitment like that." Carly always thought she'd have a wedding, but now she is coming to terms with the fact that it may never happen. "I would never say to him, 'If you never want to get married then it's over' because I would be punishing myself," she says. "What would be the purpose of that? I would rather be unmarried and be with him."

One advantage to offering an ultimatum, explains psychotherapist Dr. Jenn Berman, is that you're showing the guy you mean business. "If you're not interested in staying a relationship any longer unless someone marries you, it's smart to give him the opportunity to step up to the plate," she says. "He may not realize how important it is to you." Still, she adds, "It's not the ideal way to move into a marriage, but some men need a little more pushing than others. Some men will react terribly to that, but at least you know you tried."

BOSS LADIES

Even if you know exactly what you want from a guy, that doesn't give you the right to boss him around or issue unrealistic demands. If he's an absolute neat freak and you are not, you can't expect him all of a sudden to stop caring about organization. If he loves football and you think it's dumb, you can't stop him from being a sports fan. What if he demanded that you stop caring about purses and shoes? Also, if you don't like his friends, you shouldn't try to force him to stop spending time with them. If you're monopolizing his time to the point where he doesn't have his own life anymore, or you're making him act unlike himself, you've gone too far.

Patty and her family were devastated when her brother, Lance, married Mary Beth, a woman who kept him from seeing his relatives, would summon him home when he was out with friends, and would cry if she didn't get her way. "My brother isn't any fun anymore," says Patty. "It's really sad." Mary Beth is one of those women who think if they ask a guy to do something, he always has to agree. Or worse, they say, "He should do whatever I demand."

The purpose of a demand should be to make your relationship better, not make the other person's life miserable. If you want the man in your life to be open-minded to the things you say and you want, you must be willing to treat him the same way.

THE ART OF PERSUASION

When making demands, the trick to getting your way is to approach the situation carefully or it will backfire. Don't be passive-aggressive. If he asks you if something is wrong, don't lie—and then get mad because he doesn't know what's bothering you.

Step 1: Talk to the guy the way you would talk to a friend. Don't whine or nag. Simply state what you need, nicely, calmly, and in a matter-of-fact tone. Says relationship expert Sherry Amatenstein, "Don't speak in a way that is accusatory. Don't knock the other person." Adds Berman, "When asking a guy to do something vague like, 'Listen to me more,' it's important to give him specific instructions. The biggest mistake that most women make in a relationship is to say vague things. Describe what you mean. He may be listening, but he's not giving you the clues that you need. Say, 'Make eye contact with me and respond in ways that indicate to me that you heard what I said.' A guy can be reading the paper and feel like he's listening, and a woman will feel completely ignored even though he's heard every word you said."

If you're feeling neglected . . .
Instead of saying: "You're such an ass. You never spend time with me. You are not going out with your friends this weekend because you have to be with me."
Say: "Hey, I'm feeling like we don't see enough of each other and I miss you. I would love to spend some private time with you this weekend."

If you need him to help you around the house . . .

Instead of saying: "You're such a pig. All I ever do is clean up after you."

Say: "It would mean a lot to me if you put your dishes in the dishwasher instead of leaving them in the sink. I know you probably don't even realize you're doing it."

If you need him to be more romantic or do things for you . . .

Instead of saying: "You never do anything nice for me like bring me flowers or cook me dinner. My friend's boyfriends are always do things like that. Why don't you?"

Say: "You're such a good cook. I'd love for you to make me dinner this weekend." Positive reinforcement is key.

Liza, who has been with her husband for ten years, explains, "There's a big difference between standing up for yourself and being a shrew. Men are afraid of anger and brutal honesty. You have to be diplomatic and finesse the situation. Be the ultimate politician. You have to be aware that you could be demanding the thing that pushes the relationship over the edge, but speaking up for yourself is better than staying in a shitty relationship."

Step 2: After you've made your demand, give him time to process it and give him a chance to change. I don't even mean the guy has to change himself completely; it's just that he has to acknowledge *in his actions* that he's more aware of what you need from him.

People often don't even realize they behave a certain way until someone else points it out. As I've mentioned before, one of my exes was so preoccupied with a new job and a new apartment it was almost as if he forgot he had a girlfriend. As soon as I mentioned it, he quickly returned to the routine of calling me and coming over.

On the other hand, if you ask a guy to do something that isn't in his personality—like expect a slob to start cleaning up after himself—it isn't going to happen overnight, but he should at least show you he's making an effort. "If he's promised to change, the attempt to change should start immediately," says relationship expert Carolyn Bushong. "You should also have a system worked out where you point out when he's doing his bad behavior. He should stop and correct himself at that moment. If he gets defensive, he's probably not really going to change."

Even the smallest sign of effort might be enough to make you feel better. It's just nice to know that someone is willing to fight for you, make compromises for you, or see things from your perspective. If you're clearly communicating you're upset about something and all you get back is, "Just deal with it" (that's a quote from one of my exes), your relationship may be doomed.

Step 3: Understand that you might not always see eye to eye. Says married Francine, "I've found that what you need to let up on the most is expecting the other person to react exactly as you would. You need to realize they are a totally different person with different world experiences who come to each situation with a different point of view. It's not that you can't impact their lives in a way you'd like, or make some changes, but you need to let up on banging them on the head with it because that's not going to make them get it."

I once got annoyed with a boyfriend because I was under the impression he didn't want to meet my friends. Every time I asked him to come and join us at a bar, he'd have an excuse for why he couldn't make it. (I'd already met his friends, his father, and his sister, so I knew he wasn't ashamed of being with me.) When I told him how I felt, he explained that he *did* want to meet my friends, he was just uncomfortable being the only guy in a big group of women; it was intimidating. If I hadn't said anything about it, I would have gone on to assume he was a self-centered jerk who wasn't worth dating. As it turned out, he was just shy. All I needed to do was arrange for him to meet a smaller group. Problem solved.

It's not asking too much to have your wants and needs met by the man in your life. However, a great relationship involves a certain level of ease. You shouldn't have to exhaust yourself by constantly asking for more attention, more help, more commitment, more of anything. As Carly once learned, that is often a sign you're with the wrong man. "When I was with my ex-boyfriend,

I complained a few times, 'Can you plan things for us? We don't do anything.' Our relationship was boring, but he said he'd try and do more. When he broke up with me several months later, I thought it came out of the blue. But he explained, 'I realized that I should want to do all the things that you asked me to do and you shouldn't have to ask for them.'"

BOTTOM LINE

Always remember, there is somebody out there who will care about your feelings. In the meantime, if you choose to stay with someone who doesn't make compromises for you, you have to either accept it or get out. If you don't get out and you're still unhappy or annoyed, then the only person you can blame for your unhappiness is yourself.

Chapter Eighteen

Red Flags and Deal Breakers

*I*n 2004, *actress Halle Berry appeared on* The Oprah Win-
frey Show *and discussed her failed marriage to singer Eric
Benét. When they wed in 2001, she was unaware that he was
a sex addict. "[When] I look back at our relationship . . . I
didn't see flags of sexual addiction, but I saw the flags of something not right in a relationship early, early on," she said. "But I
wanted this relationship. I loved this man so much that I made up
in my mind it wasn't a flag." When Halle would confront her
husband about other women, he'd turn the situation around and
make her feel "insecure or needy," she explained, so she would
back off. Eventually, she came to her senses. "If I'm your committed partner . . . I have a right to know where you were at
4:00 in the morning, and that doesn't make me insecure," she
told Oprah. "It doesn't make me needy. I have a right to ask
those questions . . . and demand an answer." Her big lesson
from the experience? "I've learned that when I see a flag in a re-*

lationship next time, recognize it as a flag. Don't think, Oh, that's just a shadow."

Halle Berry: beautiful, talented, and oh so smart. As much as we all want happy endings, the way to get there is not by averting your eyes to the truth. It doesn't mean you should be paranoid, or freak out at every little thing that sets off an alarm in your head. However—I'll say it again—it's so important to trust your instincts. Pay attention to red flags because if you know what you want and need from a relationship, those flags will alert you to behavior that doesn't fit your goals. You'll save yourself time and heartache.

Red flags don't only alert you to cheating. They also point out all kinds of awful conduct, such as drug abuse, disrespect, or neglect—things you shouldn't put up with in a long-term relationship, aka deal breakers. I realized I had no future with an ex-boyfriend when he was giving his dog more love and attention than he gave me. I'll admit, I'm not a dog person—frankly, I'm a little scared of them—but I do appreciate the pet-owner bond. Still, I found it very odd when Dog Guy told me he was thinking about getting Fido's paw print tattooed on his back. But that wasn't what really bothered me. One of the first red flags went up when we were making plans to hang out one Sunday night and watch *The Sopranos*. I suggested we meet up a few hours before the show aired, and he gave me a hard time. "I can't come over that early! I need to hang out with my dog," he told me. As far as our dating schedule went, we were only seeing each other once or twice a week, so from my perspective, four hours on a Sunday wasn't asking for much. I would have understood if he needed to see his grandmother, or visit some friends, but dissed for his dog? They *live* together.

A few weeks later, I cooked an Easter dinner at Dog Guy's apartment. He was overly concerned that I was making a mess in his kitchen. (Meanwhile, his dog kept rubbing up against the freshly painted walls.) The entire time, I was also tripping over the pooch, which was following me around. When I nicely commented that he was in my way, D.G. screamed, "Fido!" and, finally, I was left alone—by the man *and* his best friend. D.G. barely spoke to me the rest of the night and acted as if he was mad at *me* because he had to say something to the dog. Red flag number two. Later in the evening, he cuddled *with Fido* and said, "I'm sorry, I've been mean to you today." I thought, You're going to apologize to the dog and you've ignored me all night? This was not the kind of relationship I deserved.

I wouldn't have wanted or expected D.G. to give up his beloved pet for me. If he'd shown me half the attention he gave that animal I would have been satisfied. But the bottom line was that this guy wasn't making me a priority. In my world, that's a deal breaker. As relationship expert Dennie Hughes later reminded me, "If he's not putting you first now, who or what is he going to put first in the future?"

SEEING RED

As we all know, a lot of red flags only show up in hindsight, but that's often because you're not paying close enough attention while the relationship is going on, or, as in Halle's case, you just choose to ignore reality. It's perfectly normal (and necessary) to question aspects of your relationship. For example, if you've been dating for a while, and he's not introducing you to his friends, you should be wondering why. If you're talking marriage, why does he refuse to give you a key to his apartment? Why will he only see you on Sundays? If you're committed to not settling, your red flag radar will be more sensitive than that of a desperate woman. You should be able to pick up on warning signs. Sharing stories with other women will help you hone your skills.

So, for what should you be on the lookout? Based on my own experiences, you're in trouble if you're with someone who is condescending or controlling. I had a boyfriend who would tell me what to wear, what to say, how to act—even what to eat. "Honey . . . ," he'd say, shaking his head as I picked up a brownie. Constructive criticism is one thing, but this was constant. The longer we dated, the worse I felt about myself. I'd tell him he was hurting my feelings, but he didn't seem to care. He felt as if everything I did was a reflection on him, so he had a right to control me. In his eyes, he thought he was helping me. (Um, I don't need to be fixed, thanks.) All of those flags were showing me that this was a completely unbalanced relationship—and one I realized was not worth continuing.

The best relationships have a give-and-take dynamic. If someone is only taking, that's another bad sign. "I recently dated a guy who never asked me any questions about myself," says Melissa. "He just really, really liked to talk about himself. At first, I tried to justify this behavior as him trying to impress me with all the great things about himself, or him being nervous and talking too much as a result. But it just never got any better. I mean, the guy wouldn't even ask me how my meal was when I had just asked him. Who doesn't ask a reciprocal question like that? 'How's your burger?' 'Good, how's your salad?' It was all about him, so I decided to leave him in his own good company. I should have done it sooner."

Indeed, we all have regrets that we've missed signs at one time or another. As private school administrator Grace, 22, recalls, "I was always told that hockey players had the worst reputation and were trouble. I knew this was all true. Then I started dating one, and the first thing he said to me was, 'Don't believe anything that you hear about me.' That should have been a red flag right there!" For her part, marketing exec Katie didn't realize how significant it was when an ex-boyfriend became upset with her when she didn't sing in church. "He ended up being way too religious for me," she says, "and he started treating me like a sinner for doing something silly, like wearing sexy tall black boots. I should have caught on a lot earlier than I did!" Another of her exes, whom she considered "fiscally responsible," had her chauffeur him around town because he was too cheap to buy a car. "These were nice men who had nice qualities," she says, "so if I hadn't been blinded by the hopes that the relationships would work out, I might have realized how wrong they were sooner."

More Red Flags

+ He goes out a lot with his friends and doesn't want to include you. (Bear in mind, however, that a guy has to have *some* freedom. You can't be jealous of everything he does that doesn't include you.)

+ He waits to see what his friends are doing before he makes plans with you.

+ He talks about his ex-girlfriend all the time. (This happened to Melanie: "I was trying to be nice and let him talk about it," she explains. "He ended up getting back together with her.")

+ He has no backbone.

+ He never, ever asks you out.

+ He's rude.

+ He lives with his parents. (Trust me, he will never put you first.)

+ He's dishonest. (A classic example? "I ignored it when a guy told me he only had two kids and then two more mysteriously appeared," says Amy. "It was all downhill from there.")

✦ When you're on a date, he always answers his cell phone.

According to relationship expert Dr. Jenn Berman, additional red flags include "not following through with his word, a bad temper, name-calling in a fight, and extreme jealousy—which is often a sign of someone who will turn out to be physically abusive. And any man who isolates you from your friends and family is bad news." Meanwhile, Carole Lieberman, M.D., a Beverly Hills psychiatrist and author of *Bad Boys: Why We Love Them, How to Live with Them, and When to Leave Them,* warns, "The biggest red flag in a romantic relationship is when the woman has a bad relationship with her father or the man has a bad relationship with his mother. They will bring these unfinished problems into their romantic relationships."

Well, if that's the biggest, then this is the most obvious: "If you find yourself continually finding things to do other than spend time with your boyfriend," says Natalie, "that's a pretty big warning sign."

EYES WIDE OPEN

If you notice a red flag, don't turn a blind eye or let a guy manipulate you into thinking you're imagining things. If you're confident and levelheaded—and not

afraid to be single—you'll be able to sort out your insecurities from his bad behavior. You must confront
him—and then see how he reacts. Does he address the
problem and make you feel better? Or does he turn
around and blame you for being needy/crazy? If so, consider that a warning sign. Also, if you suspect a man is
being unfaithful, you shouldn't snoop, although if you
feel the need, that's a red flag, too. If you can't trust a
guy (even if he's not misbehaving), then the relationship
isn't right. Either there's a reason you don't have faith in
him, he's not giving you a reason to trust him, or he's
simply bringing out the worst in you. All. Red. Flags.

Often, if things seem wrong, they probably are.
While my friend Mandy was dating Michael, he bought
a condo, and she helped him decorate it from top to bottom. She assumed they would eventually be living there
together, and yet, he refused to give her a key. Mandy
was upset but didn't want to make a big deal out of it.
She couldn't see this was a major sign of trouble, but I
did. When I tried to point out his behavior was suspi-
cious, she acted defensive and got angry *with me*. Even
tually, we found out why he didn't want her to have
access to his pad: He was cheating on her.

At least Mandy recognized that as a deal breaker.
Sarah L., on the other hand, had infidelity thrown in
her face and she still overlooked it. "I once walked in on
a boyfriend in bed with another girl," she recalls, "and
after a big fight, I still went back to him. Pathetic!"

If you stay with a man once he's proven he's not

good enough for you, you're settling. Lea admits she ignored red flags during many relationships just because she didn't want to be on her own. "In the back of my head I knew that the person I was with couldn't be The One due to the fact that he was either a bad drunk, had anger issues or jealousy issues, or was bad at socializing. I just put the red flag thoughts to the back of my head because I was in a comfortable routine. I wasn't ready for it to end." Although she believes you need to give a guy a chance to prove himself, she also realizes, "If you give too many chances, you're not being true to yourself."

DEAL OR NO DEAL

Red flags may indicate problems, but they don't automatically signal the end of a relationship. Sometimes, the issue can be resolved; other times, you discover it's really not an issue at all. Deal breakers, on the other hand, are absolutes. They are actions and/or behaviors that are so completely unacceptable to you that continuing a relationship is usually impossible and always ill-advised. According to the Lifetime Television Pulse Poll, the reasons women most often cited for a breakup were the guy "couldn't commit" (28 percent), "cheated or had wandering eyes" (26 percent), and was "more into himself than me" (21 percent). Naturally, you need to have enough self-esteem to see the reality and save yourself. Annie once dated a man she describes as "a jealous, road-raging freakazoid" and admits, "At first I thought the jealousy bit was a compliment. I was so wrong."

While there are many universal deal breakers (physical and mental abuse top the list) they also tend to vary from person to person. I will not, under any circumstances, be in a relationship with a guy who treats me disrespectfully. My friend Elizabeth agrees and adds that a man can't be unreliable, either. "If he tells you he is going to call and he doesn't, or if he inappropriately makes fun of you in front of his friends, there is no compromise," she says. "If you can't count on him and if he doesn't lift you up, don't waste your time. There are enough hardships and snags that we encounter in life on a daily basis. Why allow someone else to add to the load?"

That's certainly how Ashley felt when she reached the limit in her troubled marriage. She recalls, "The day we found out my father was going to die, I called my now ex-husband. He didn't offer to fly out of town to be with me for the news, so I asked him to be available for my phone call with test results between 4 and 6 P.M. When the surgeon gave us the prognosis, I called and called him and couldn't reach him." Where was he? "He had decided to get a ninety-minute massage at 4:30," she says. After that incident and more insensitive behavior at her father's funeral, she says, "I realized that my well-being was never going to be a priority for him and that he would never be able to take care of me or love me the way I needed to be loved. I would always have to take care of myself and be independent. We would never be a team. That was my deal breaker."

When a guy shows you that he doesn't want to be with you (in word or in deed), it's time to walk away. "In my last relationship, the deal breaker was when my boyfriend of eighteen months, with whom I was madly in love—to the point where the red flags looked like exciting challenges to my addled psyche—told me that he was 'ambivalent' about a future with me," says Sarah T. "That was the end. I told him I knew I could do better than 'ambivalent.' In retrospect, his general self-absorption and only sporadic kindness should have been the deal breakers—and in the future they will be."

More Deal Breakers

+ Physical or mental abuse (because this can't be said enough)
+ Drug or alcohol abuse
+ Lying or cheating
+ Apathy
+ Refusal to commit
+ Lack of romance/sexual chemistry
+ Lack of motivation

If you can't figure out if something is a deal breaker, refer to your list of wants and needs. If it contradicts your relationship requirements, you have your answer.

BOTTOM LINE

If you're not afraid of being single, you'll have your eyes open in a relationship. You won't be so desperate that you allow yourself to be disrespected or played for a fool. Don't ignore red flags and don't settle for deal-breaking behavior.

Chapter Nineteen

It's Not You, It's Us

W hen it comes to breakups, *Ashley confesses, "I am awful. I am an avoider. If I have only gone out with a guy
once or twice, I will just not answer my phone, not return phone
calls or e-mails, and avoid running into him." Her disappearing
act, she says, "will make me sick to my stomach. It makes me
hate myself. It would be so much better if I could just have 'the
conversation,' but I am a big baby. I have had many guys sitting on the front steps to my house because they just want an
answer. My avoidance makes it so much worse."*

No one likes to be dumped, but for many women,
it's almost worse to be the one doing the dumping.
They're overly concerned with how the guy is going to
feel, preferring instead to prolong their own suffering.
Some worry they may never find anyone else, so they
learn to cope. Others give themselves reasons why the
breakup can't happen right away. They waste their time.
They settle.

I used to be a lot like Ashley, but going on *The Bachelorette* forced me out of my breakup (dis)comfort zone. Instead of the Ashley-style "Fade Out"—which obviously doesn't work when you're surrounded by cameras—I had to deliver the news face-to-face. And after twenty-five rejections, I now consider myself a breakup master. That doesn't mean I think it's easy or fun—although giving an ass the heave-ho is always a welcome relief. More often than not, I said good-bye to nice, normal guys with whom I just had no chemistry. I've done a lot of that off the show, too. (Who hasn't?)

The first few times I had to give the farewell speech I was incredibly nervous. I practiced what I was going to say a thousand times and couldn't even look the guy in the eye when it came to having the conversation. But by the end of the show, I was able to go on live television, in front of a studio audience of strangers, and tell Jerry our relationship was over.

So what's my secret? I've learned not to think of breakups as personal affronts. As far as I'm concerned, if I'm not getting what I want and need (same goes for a man), and nothing about that is going to change, we're clearly not meant to be together. It's not so much about the guy, it's about the two of us: As a couple, we just don't work. (Granted, he may not always see it that way.) It's a simple truth. As psychotherapist Dr. Jenn Berman notes, "We're not compatible with most people." Thinking about relationships that way alleviates so much anxiety when it's time to let someone go.

BREAKUP BASICS

Every relationship is different, and so is every breakup. Before you do the deed, try to figure out why the relationship isn't working. Is it about red flags, or deal breakers? If you're the one causing the issues, make an effort to correct your behavior; for example, as I've gotten older, I've realized I need to be more laid-back and less critical. If it's not your fault, either find a way to work it out (communication is key), or get out. Here are my three most important rules for letting someone go

Rule #1: Treat the Person How You'd Want to Be Treated. According to a Happen/Match.com poll, 19 percent of men and women break up by ending contact with no explanation (aka the Fade Out). When I did that, I was always glad to avoid the awkwardness of telling a guy I didn't want to see him anymore, but the guilt—and, perhaps, bad karma—that came along with the blow off still haunts me to this day. If you know how bad you feel when a guy just disappears after a few dates, why wouldn't he feel the same? Similarly, would you want to date someone who didn't want to be with you? If not, then don't stay with a guy you don't like. "You can let a guy down in a caring way," says Elizabeth. "Frogs have feelings, too."

Rule #2: Do It Face-to-Face—or at Least Voice-to-Voice. The most mature and polite way to tell someone you're through is in person. "Even though it is the most awkward, it shows respect," explains relationship expert Dr. Carole Lieberman.

Etiquette experts might not agree with me, but I'm of the mind-set that if you've only gone out a few times, it's okay to tell a guy over the phone that you don't want to see him again—provided you call him while he's at home (not at work or in the car), and you actually get him on the phone. A voice mail breakup is bad form.

One delivered via e-mail is even worse. According to a Match.com survey of more than four thousand single men and women, almost 50 percent of them have been on the sending or receiving end of a breakup message. (Who can even predict how many of those have been forwarded to friends?) I'll be honest: I've sent a couple myself. It's such a bad idea. One guy started an e-mail war with me, bombarding me with long messages every fifteen minutes, even before I had time to respond. Another guy didn't even reply to my breakup e-mail, leaving me wondering what he thought. Was he pissed? Did he agree? Did he hate me? I had no closure.

While I would never do that again, I have found that writing down my thoughts is a good pre-breakup strategy. It can help you sort out your feelings and plan what you want to say in your breakup speech. Compose a letter or an e-mail—just don't send it. It worked for Lea when she decided to end a two-and-a-half-year relationship. She recalls, "I gave my boyfriend a letter in person, then talked it through with him. We have remained good friends."

Rule #3: Be Honest. As the old saying goes, "The truth shall set you free." If you don't see your relationship going anywhere, speak up. If your personalities don't mesh, say so. If you think he's great but just not great for you, tell him. My parting words to John Paul: "I think you have every quality I look for in someone, but . . . something is just not there." Men still want to hear the truth about why they're being dumped. Tough as they may seem, they need closure just as much as we do.

Naturally, what you tell someone you've been casually dating will be different from what you tell a long-term boyfriend. If you haven't established a close, committed relationship, it's fine to stay general. Twenty-seven percent of daters say, "You're a great person, but I don't see a fit between us." It's honest, and certainly more tactful than saying, "I can't date you because I think you're a loser and you gross me out." Blair recalls a creative brush-off she received from a guy she'd dated for about a month: "He called me and said, 'I just wanted to tell you, I'm going to be very busy.' That was it. There was no 'But let's get together when things slow down.' Just 'busy.' I realized he was telling me he wouldn't have time to see me forever. I was a little puzzled by the call, but afterward, I started to appreciate the line. My feelings weren't hurt at all."

If you're dissatisfied with a relationship that has been going on for a while, you owe it to the guy to offer a more detailed explanation. In fact, the breakup shouldn't come out of the blue; if you've been having issues, you should have been discussing them. Lieberman's suggested script: "This relationship just isn't working for me anymore. I find I'm miserable more often than happy. I've tried telling you about the things I see as problems, but now I've come to the conclusion that we just need to end our relationship, so we can each be happier."

If what you're saying isn't truthful, the other person is going to sense it. "Everybody knows when you are feeding them a line," says Jamie, a fan of "gentle honesty." If you make up some big, convoluted story about why you're breaking up, it just makes things unnecessarily complicated. When Corinne broke things off with the guy she met through her grandmother, she lied and told him she was still interested in her ex-boyfriend, and even added that he might be moving back to town. "Then, I had to call my mother and tell her what I'd said, in case word got back to my grandmother," explains Corinne. "My grandmother, of course, did ask about the ex. I continued to lie. It made a bad situation even worse."

MAKE IT QUICK

Breaking up is like ripping off a Band-Aid: It's going to hurt, but if you do it quickly, it's much less painful. That doesn't mean looking at a guy, blurting out, "Idon'twant todateyouanymore," and running for the door. But when you know it's time for the relationship to end, don't delay. Says Amy, "I cut to the chase and say 'bye-bye.' I'd rather be honest and direct so there isn't a need for closure down the road." I often hear people say, "I'm just going to give it another month. By then it will be easier." Why? Why is a month going to make it any easier? You'll only be building up resentment and wasting time. Let's face it, there's never a good time to tell a guy you don't want to be with him. The sooner you do it, the sooner you can both move on.

Dina admits she once dragged out a past relationship "because there were times when everything was great." You have to see a relationship for what it is on the whole, not just during the good times. "It took me leaving on an international trip and developing feelings for someone else to realize I had to terminate the relationship," she says. "And even then, it was his birthday when I got back into town, so I had to wait another couple of weeks. He was a good person and I wanted to soften the blow as much as I could. But there's nothing you can do when you don't love someone back."

A word about timing: Yes, it is wrong to break a person's heart on their birthday, when they've just gotten other bad news, or any other day of the year that holds special significance. However, if you know you want to break up with a man, don't go on vacation with him or attend a family event (his or yours) together. On *The Bachelorette,* I was forced into those situations, and it was always so uncomfortable. Not only is it a waste of time, but you're also giving the guy—and other people—the wrong impression about the status of your relationship. It's also rude to allow yourself to be wined and dined by family members if the next day (or week) you're going to call it quits. Instead of hurting only the man's feelings, you end up burning bridges with his entire family.

Don't feel so bad for a guy (or worry so much about what his family and friends will think of you) that you stay in the relationship out of pity. I did it once, and I know how agonizing it can be. When I broke up with him, he begged me not to end it. For a moment, I even thought about reconsidering because I hated seeing him so sad. But that's no reason to date a person.

Several years before she married, Rebecca had a nine-month relationship with Ted. He was very sweet and soft-spoken—and very unhappy with his life. "He didn't like his job, he didn't like his friends, and he'd gained a lot of weight," she remembers. "So many things were miserable for him." Gone was the friendly, upbeat personality that drew Rebecca to Ted in the first place. Now, he was depressed and cranky. Rebecca grew less excited about the relationship as each day passed, but she stayed in it for Ted's sake. "I was afraid I'd add to his misery if I broke up with him. I felt bad because I felt like all of his happiness was derived from me. But people have to be happy with themselves to be successful in a relationship. Finally, I realized I had to end it, especially because I already had a crush on another guy."

As awful as you may feel about breaking up, you can't let a man's well-being take precedence over yours. Some people may call that selfish, but if you don't want to settle, think of it as self-preservation.

There are times you might even be agonizing for no reason at all. "I have found that most of the time, the guy will know you are about to break up with him because you have been acting differently," says Grace. "Every time I've broken up with a guy he has told me that he sees it coming." In fact, he could be feeling the same way as you and you don't even know it. "I dated a guy in college for three years," Sarah L. tells me. "Things were never really great. We were always fighting. When I finally got up the nerve to just end it, I figured I'd send out a message by not calling him anymore. And you know what? He just stopped calling me, too. And that is how we broke up! No conversation, no fight, no tears. We just each stopped on our own—after three years!"

LIFE GOES ON

When I have trouble mustering up the courage to end a relationship, I remind myself this: If I am confident the right man is out there for me, I know there will be another woman for him. People made such a stink when I didn't choose certain men from *The Bachelorette,* but I never once felt like their lives would be over once they left the show. I'm sure they've all moved on. Andrew, as well, has found love since we split. Men's hearts do get broken, but none of them are going to die (nor will you) or run out of chances for love just because one woman doesn't want to be with them.

Still, it's hard to let go when you've become close

friends—although that's even more reason to do it. Don't you want what's best for your friends? Would you want a girlfriend to be in a bad relationship? Letting go is more difficult in these circumstances, but it's best for both of you. "I thought I had found the love of my life, and even when the flame died, I wanted to try to make it work," says Daniele. "We both did, actually. We discovered that we were hanging on to the idea of being the perfect couple, when we really were not fulfilled in the relationship. We eventually decided to stop the madness and are friends today." If you don't seize the urge to end a relationship, the consequences could be worse than anything you could have said in your breakup conversation. "I was living with someone who was 100 percent not right for me and I knew it, but we'd become so close—brother-sister close, not romantically close—that the idea of separating our lives seemed inconceivable," recalls Sarah T. "So I started sleeping with other people. I used my cheating as an escape hatch. He was devastated."

BOTTOM LINE

You deserve to be happy, and sometimes that does mean hurting a guy's feelings. In the long run, it will be better for the both of you. The guy will survive and he will get over it. Doesn't he deserve to be with someone who really loves him? If you break it off, you're truly doing both of you a favor.

Chapter Twenty

Get Over It

I have different stages *of getting over a breakup,"* Valerie tells me. *"Initially, I cry. I don't eat—it's a fabulous diet. I talk my friends to death about the topic. It's like any loss. You go through denial, anger, and that hopeful stage where you think it will work out." Her reaction, however, also depends on which end of the split she finds herself. "When I break up with some-one, I need to be out all the time, drinking a lot and partying a lot and letting off steam. If someone is breaking up with me, I turn into a recluse. Recovery is getting easier, though," she says. "Men are a dime a dozen. In the grand scheme of things, it's not a real loss. It's just a guy."*

Breakups aren't the end of the world, but there's no denying they stink. As great as it is to be single, for most of us, the ultimate goal is to meet the right guy, get married, and start a family. Every split sends us hurtling back to square one. You have a right to be sad and disappointed—just not forever. The only way you're ever going to fulfill your goal is to pick yourself up off the couch and get on with your life.

Every split has a different recovery time, depending on the circumstances. I've dated a lot of people, but only three breakups have had major impacts. I was with my college boyfriend for four years, and we broke up four months after graduation. I was upset, but given that I was young and starting a new chapter in my life, and he was living seven hundred miles away, the adjustment wasn't too hard. The future was so exciting that it was nearly impossible for me to hang on to the past.

My next big split, with Andrew, was an entirely different story. There was so much involved in the relationship—from deciding to be on the show to my move to San Francisco—that I had a lot to process in the end. I'd always hoped we'd have a perfect fairy-tale ending to our crazy love story, so not only did I have to cope with not being with Andrew anymore, but I also mourned the loss of what we were supposed to have. (Of course, it's so easy to idealize things in hindsight; while we were together, I was often miserable.)

Bouncing back from my last serious relationship took a good couple of months. I wasn't crying about it right away; in fact, it was somewhat of a relief. Our relationship attracted a lot of attention (he was my first post-*Bachelorette* boyfriend), so when it was over, I was glad to finally relax. When it settled in that we weren't going to have a future together, that's when I got really sad.

It's natural to have down moments and down days,

even after months have passed since the relationship ended. But it's more constructive to focus on enjoying life as it is rather than wishing for something you don't have.

RECOVERY EFFORTS

Some people will tell you that the best remedy for a breakup is to go do something productive to get your mind off things. What do I consider productive? Calling up a friend who disliked the guy the most, and talking to her about my drama for an hour. (What doesn't help is talking to people who only admit *after* the breakup, "I never liked him anyway." Oh great, *now* you tell me? Or worse, those who ask, "Why does this keep happening to you?" Uh, thanks. Comments like those only make things worse; you feel sad *and* stupid.) I also believe in getting mad and/or sulking for a day or two . . . or a few weeks . . . maybe even a few months—whatever it takes. Meanwhile, nothing is more satisfying than deleting an ex's phone number and e-mail address.

My recovery process is always much quicker if I don't keep my emotions bottled up inside. Sometimes, I'll find an inspiring theme song and play the hell out of it. A recent favorite: "Since You've Been Gone" by Kelly Clarkson. Call me cheesy, but the lyrics ("I'm so moving on/Yeah Yeah") remind me that I'm better off without the guy. I also love "Single" by Natasha Bedingfield, and "I Don't Need a Man" by the Pussycat Dolls.

If I need to release some anger, I head to a kickboxing class and fantasize that I'm punching my ex. (It also helps to imagine seeing the look on his face when he catches a glimpse of your toned, post-breakup body.) Another mind trick: Think about the bad parts of a relationship—the fights, the exhaustion, the neglect. I miss it less when it seems so horrible.

Any woman who has been through a few breakups knows what it takes to get herself out of the funk. Says Melanie, "Mostly, an insane amount of dwelling on everything that was said and done throughout the course of the relationship, how I have been wronged, and ways I wronged that person." Rebecca always preferred the couch potato approach. "I liked to lie around in my pajamas, watch TV, and eat shitty food," she recalls. "And then I would bounce back. But I needed time to wallow and obsess." Annie's remedies: "One-night stands, Dove bars, *Sex and the City,* Oprah, self-help books, Bally's— in that order." Rachel says she writes "long, dramatic e-mails," but never ends up sending them. "Thank God," she adds. "Another thing I'll do is fixate on the things that were really gross about the guy—like he didn't own a real bed, just a mattress, or he said 'Alls you gotta do.' And I'll also vent and whine to a friend until she can no longer take it, then I'll move on to others until there's no one left to talk to. Then I'm over it."

Melissa, who has survived three years of bad relationships, says one way she gets over it is by analyzing the relationship. "It's cathartic," she says. "And when you've analyzed until you can analyze no more, come to terms with the fact that you will probably never get the answers you crave. Be okay with the mystery never being solved. It really doesn't matter anyway."

Even psychiatrist Carole Lieberman advocates indulging your sorrows—at least temporarily. As she puts it, "The best way to get over a breakup is by eating rocky road ice cream, crying, staying in bed watching TV or reading books—until you're done or until life necessitates your getting out of bed. Then you can start doing things with friends and socializing again."

RECONNECT

Friends, as a matter of fact, are an integral part of getting over any breakup. Provided you didn't dump them when you got into your relationship (such a no-no), they will be the ones who will listen, make you laugh, sympathize, empathize, and drag you out against your will but for your own good. (And by all means, go *out* with them; don't sit inside chatting every night.) Says self-proclaimed breakup expert Melissa, "Surround yourself with friends and family who know how fabulous you are and know how much you deserve. You'll be reminded of how much you're loved and that there are people in your life who love you for who you are." Adds Sarah L., "Really, time is the only thing that helps get over a split—and having great friends to be there to support you."

When Andrew and I were having problems, it was so

comforting to know that there were, in fact, people in the world who understood me and valued me. I wasn't scared about the breakup because I knew I wasn't going to be alone. In fact, when I moved back to Chicago from San Francisco, I crashed with friends while I found a new apartment. I love living solo, but roommates came in very handy at that time. Had I been on my own, I would have spent every waking moment thinking about the split and rehashing the whole thing in my head over and over again. My friends kept me occupied and optimistic—especially when so many people (strangers) were telling me I'd never do any better than Andrew.

Don't try to get over a guy by yourself. You have to be willing to lean on people—even professionals, as Sarah T. discovered after a particularly rough split. "I'd frankly encourage anyone else who's tried time alone, jumping back in, exercise, vacations, job changes, moving, etc., and *still* can't get out of a slump, to hit the shrink's office. Sometimes we just need help with this kind of stuff," she says. "It's good to learn to be alone and to be happy, but we don't have to be either of those things all the time, and we don't have to figure out how to do it all by ourselves."

USE THIS TIME FOR YOU

In addition to spending time with your friends, you also need to schedule time for yourself. Revel in your new-found freedom. "Take a time-out and stay busy," says relationship expert Dennie Hughes. "Take a class you've always thought about, sign up for a self-improvement course, volunteer—it's an eye opener. How can you wallow when you are seeing others who have things worse than you?" I may be sad when a relationship is over, but I also love that I don't have to consider someone else's schedule when I make plans. And when I go shopping, I can buy whatever I like and don't have to worry about what my ex will think about it. After living with Andrew in *his* apartment, I was so excited to have the freedom to choose where I wanted to live and to have a job of my own choosing. As I reclaimed my life, I gained confidence.

We all come out of relationships as changed women. Spend time getting reacquainted with yourself and who you have become. Focus on the future. "When I didn't take time to be alone," says Daniele, "I found myself dwelling on the past relationship, and it seemed like everything around me triggered memories of it."

FIND ANOTHER GUY

After singer Sheryl Crow and cyclist Lance Armstrong called off their engagement in 2006, she appeared on *The Ellen DeGeneres Show* and said, "My friends say I have to get back on the bike, and I keep saying—maybe not the bike." Her friends used the wrong analogy, but they definitely had the right idea: One surefire way to get over one guy is to find another. That was my motivation behind going on *The Bachelorette*. I didn't even have to think about where, when, or how I would meet other men. Signing on to the show automatically gave me something to which I could look forward. Instead of dwelling on what could have been, I took charge of my life and put myself right back out in the dating world. "The quickest way to get over a breakup is another relationship," explains Lieberman. "But this is tricky, since you don't want to go into another relationship on the rebound, before you've finished mourning the last one." Indeed, if you rush back into the singles scene and only encounter losers, you might end up wishing you were back with the ex. Says Liz, "I think you're doomed to obsess about your last relationship—no matter how bad it was—until the next one comes along. Of course, it's best to just jump back in if you have the opportunity."

Some women, however, are willing to take that risk and believe that jumping back in to the dating world is the only way to get over a failed relationship. "I'm a big advocate of the rebound guy if you can find the right one," admits Natalie. "Fresh out of a relationship, you need to have a testosterone fix of some sort. If you can find some guy who is handsome and lots of fun—but you don't make out with him—it's very therapeutic." She quickly adds, "Sexual rebound guys are fun, too." (Still, you're better off keeping things PG until you're out of any kind of fragile emotional state. You don't need to give yourself any more issues.)

SEE WHAT'S OUT THERE

People may have snickered when I decided to be on *The Bachelorette,* but knowing there were going to be *twenty-five* men handpicked for me helped combat feelings that I might never meet another guy. Online dating sites serve a similar purpose. "You see how many people are out there," explains Katie. Adds Lisa, "There's always an opportunity to meet or connect with someone 24/7." And Heather notes, "Having someone younger telling you you're stunning and he can't believe you are your age makes you smile a bit." When Joanie's marriage ended, she found online dating helped her brush up on skills she hadn't used in years. "I got back into the swing of things," she tells me. "It was really *a lot* of fun. Even the bad dates were hilarious stories for my next girls' night out! Cheapskates, the clear pothead, the man who only talked about himself, the sex fiend—I enjoyed myself completely. If you figure that it's meant to be fun, and sort of a buffet where you get to try things out, then the pressure is way off." Olivia agrees: "I loved the attention and it was a total distraction." Where not to go looking for men when you're feeling down? "A bar," says Katie. "It makes you feel like there is *no one* worth finding."

AVOID TEMPTATION

No matter how grim the dating pool seems, resist temptation to reconnect with your ex. "Don't call, don't write, no text messages," advises psychotherapist Dr. Jen Berman. "Anytime you see him again, you are tearing the scab off the wound and you can expect it to bleed a lot." Even if you're over him, he might not be over you. Either way, someone is bound to get hurt.

Blair (foolishly) met up with an ex-boyfriend for lunch seven months after they broke up. "I thought it would be fine," she says. "He was visiting from out of town and I figured it would give me some closure." Lunch turned into an afternoon, which turned into evening plans. "I was really having fun with him. It was like old times. He even said how he thought we'd still be together if we didn't live in different cities." But by the end of the night, she remembered why she broke up with him. "All of his issues started to resurface. He was so insecure. And he was sending me so many mixed messages, acting like he was into me one minute and then pulling away the next. I couldn't believe I let him play me like that again." Incidents like that do have one benefit: They remind you why you're not still a couple. Unbelievably, Blair met the same guy for drinks when he moved back to her town a few years later. "I don't know what I was thinking. Maybe I was holding out hope that things would be different. I thought he'd be more mature and nicer. I thought we could be friends. Of course, he tried to make it something more, and then screwed me over—again! I would have been so much better off never taking his calls after the initial breakup. I thought I was being mature by not holding a grudge, but that's exactly what I should have done. It would have spared me a lot of mental anguish."

I've been able to remain on friendly terms with some of my old boyfriends (as in, I wouldn't turn and run if I saw them), but it took many months of limited to no contact to get to that point. Even now, I'm not calling any of them to make plans. And I try to avoid hearing about their love lives, not because I don't wish them well, but because I don't want to create any kind of competition in my head. You should never get into a relationship just to spite an ex or make him jealous. Live and love for *you*.

ON THE MEND

It's been said that time heals all wounds, but broken hearts can take awhile. According to a *Cosmopolitan* online poll of more than ten thousand people, 28.4 percent said it took them "longer than a year" to get over their last ex. The most popular healing time: "a few months" (31.7 percent). Nearly a quarter of the respondents said, "As long as it took to meet the next guy." As Dina explains, "If I've emotionally exited a relationship a long time before the breakup, then it is easy to just start dating right away. If I had real feelings for someone and he ended it, it's hard to move on because I'm comparing new people to him, seeing if they measure up."

In some cases, a split can be so devastating that you may never truly get over it. (This tends to happen a lot when the relationship doesn't end well, or you disagree with the reason for the breakup.) But even though you may always feel a little pang in your heart, you still have to be able to move on. Not being over it in weeks is okay; feeling like life is over is not. "I don't think I ever get over the people who have hurt me," admits Valerie. "I don't know if it's them that I haven't gotten over, or that I didn't get a fair shot at the relationship. They ended it too early for me to know. They always have a piece of me. Maybe I'm never over it, but I can move on." Mandy was utterly distraught when she and Mi-chael broke up, but she's finally reached a point where she's not hung up on him like she used to be. (It helps that she's madly in love with her current boyfriend.) "It took two years to fully recover," she says. "I decided it's not something I'm going to spend the rest of my life be-ing sad about."

I've been in relationships where I thought I was on the road to marriage. After the breakups, I'd wonder if I'd ever feel that way again. I'd also think if my ex dated someone else, I'd die. But that feeling has gone away over time. I've dated other people. Life goes on. The worst mistake you can make is to think you won't do better. It's natural to get scared and feel panicked, but someone always does come along.

THINK POSITIVE

You can be sad about a breakup, but always try to look on the bright side. Carly tells me, "I woke up from my last breakup thinking, This is so exciting! I never thought I'd ever have a first kiss again." When sales manager Maggie, 35, got divorced, she sold her rings and bought herself something she'd always wanted: breast implants. "It wasn't about him anymore," she explains, "it was about me."

Helen couldn't wait to get on with her life when her ex-husband moved out of their apartment. "I took everything in the apartment that was essentially his and I offered to deliver it to him," she says. "Then I went out and bought stuff that suited my taste and what I wanted. I bought dishes, knives. It was like a divorce registry. Now, when I wake up, it's wonderful. Every time I look around the apartment, it's like, Wow, this really is my own life. I'm so excited to live the life *I* want to live. I feel independent."

BOTTOM LINE

If you find yourself single again, don't sweat it. There's so much to be happy about. Be relieved that you didn't settle. And be proud of yourself for being strong enough to move on. You're better off on your own than with someone who doesn't love you or whom you don't love. "When you're done feeling bad, it's very liberating," says Rebecca. "It feels so good. You see new opportunities. It's like putting on a pair of sunglasses with tinted lenses."

Epilogue

In my original book proposal, this chapter was titled "Good Things Come to Those Who Wait." At the time, I was in a relationship that I thought (or at least hoped) would last forever. I was going to tell you how, compared with all of my past relationships, this one felt right, and how all of the challenges I've faced finally paid off. It would have made for a pretty perfect ending.

Instead, I'm single—and, in a way, I have the book to thank for that. I don't mean that in a negative way, either. As I was writing about everything women should expect from a relationship, I started to realize that my own situation wasn't meeting my standards. My boyfriend wasn't there for me in the ways I wanted and needed him to be (and he wasn't about to change). When I was thinking about women who transform themselves to suit a man, all I had to do was look in the mirror to find an example of someone who had done it.

Also, interviewing former settlers Joanie, Ashley, and Fay was a great wake-up call. I didn't want to end up telling a similar story years from now. I imagine my relationship would have ended even without this book, but the constant reminder that we're all better off single than sorry sped up the process. I have no regrets.

Four other guys came and went as the writing process continued. Once again, I lived by the book's message. I knew pretty early on that none of them were right for me, so I made sure I didn't drag out those relationships longer than necessary. And I didn't just have my own girlfriends encouraging me to hold out for the right guy, I also had all of the women who shared their stories. Knowing there are like-minded people are out there assured me I wasn't being crazy or foolish for preferring to be single than dating a man I didn't like. I have no doubt the waiting will eventually pay off.

It did for one woman you met in the book: Rachel, who had been single for two years, finally found someone who doesn't make her vomit or treat her badly. Her new boyfriend is attentive and sweet and makes her feel good about herself. "He's amazing!" she says to anyone who will listen. "Now I know I shouldn't have been wasting time on guys who didn't like me."

I know my "good thing" is out there. And if for some reason it takes awhile to find him, I will be okay. My triantapentaphobia is in check, thanks to the conversations I had with Candice and Pam. They made me feel so much more relaxed about my future.

For now, I'm going to revel in my singleness. I'm going to be thankful that I'm not in an unhappy relationship. I'm going to live my life to the fullest and never sit around feeling sorry for myself. Why should I? After all, it's great to be single. You can do what you want, when you want, how you want. You can flirt without repercussions. The list goes on and on. The best reason of all? There's a sense that any minute, you can be swept off your feet.

Acknowledgments

First, I need to thank all the men who have come in and out of my life, my friends' lives, and friends of friends' lives. You gave us more than enough material for this book and for that I am grateful.

To my family—Mom, Dad, and Jason—thank you for always being there for me, especially through the many ups and downs over the last few years. You have always loved and supported me unconditionally and are my biggest cheerleaders. I love you and thank you for always being on my side. I wouldn't be where I am today without you.

To my best friends—Lauren, Michelle, Shawn, and Julie—you are my second family and I don't know how I'd get through life, single or otherwise, without you.

To my fabulous team of agents—Pilar Queen, Richard Pine, and Matthew Guma—for taking a chance on me, patiently answering my endless questions, and guiding me throughout this entire process. Thank you to my lawyer, Richard Heller, for taking me on and steering me in the right direction. Thank you to my editor, Sarah Durand, and everyone at William Morrow for looking beyond my "reality-TV-show past" and believing in this message and in this project.

B—thank you for encouraging me to go after this, leading me to the right people, and helping me accomplish this goal.

Thank you to all of the wonderful women who contributed to this book. I'm thrilled that you were willing to talk to me and be so candid. Your stories inspired me, and I know they'll inspire others.

Many thanks to all the experts who contributed, especially Dennie Hughes, Dr. Jenn Berman, Dr. Carole Lieberman, Carolyn Bushong, Dr. Debbie Then, Dr. Robi Ludwig, Dr. Abby Roth, and Sherry Amatenstein. Thank you for your brilliant insights and expertise.

And, most important, an enormous thank you to Joey Bartolomeo for all your hard work and dedication to this project. You helped turn my crazy thoughts into words, and I couldn't be happier with the outcome. You are so talented, and you challenged me to always work harder and think harder; I can't imagine what this would have become without you. Thank you so much, and I hope we get to do it again soon.